W9-BAX-072

THE
REFERENCE
SHELF

SUICIDE

Edited by ROBERT EMMET LONG

THE REFERENCE SHELF

Volume 67 Number 2

THE H. W. WILSON COMPANY

New York   1995

THE REFERENCE SHELF

The books in this series contain reprints of articles, excerpts from books, and addresses on current issues and social trends in the United States and other countries. There are six separately bound numbers in each volume, all of which are generally published in the same calendar year. One number is a collection of recent speeches; each of the others is devoted to a single subject and gives background information and discussion from various points of view, concluding with a comprehensive bibliography that contains books and pamphlets and abstracts of additional articles on the subject. Books in the series may be purchased individually or on subscription.

Library of Congress Cataloging-in-Publication Data

Suicide / edited by Robert Emmet Long.
    p.   cm. — (Reference shelf ; v. 67. no. 2)
    Includes bibliographical references.
    ISBN 0-8242-0869-2
    1. Suicide.   2. Teenagers—Suicidal Behavior.   3. Right to die.
4. Assisted suicide.   I. Long, Robert Emmet.   II. Series.
HV6545.S815   1995
362.2'8—dc20   95-11850
                                                          CIP

Cover: Group of mourners at a funeral in Florida.

Photo: AP/Wide World Photos

Printed in the United States of America

CONTENTS

IV. KEVORKIAN'S CRITICS

BIBLIOGRAPHY

During the last decade suicide has been an increasing reality of American life, especially for adolescents, among whom the rate of suicide has tripled. Because of the stresses of growing up—including neglect and child abuse—teenagers today often experience disillusionment early. At the other end of the spectrum, adults who are terminally ill and the elderly have in some cases chosen to end their lives with dignity rather than to continue in intolerable pain and to be a burden to others. The right-to-die issue was dramatized in the case of Nancy Cruzan, who lapsed into an irreversible coma, and whose feeding tube was eventually removed by court order, allowing her to die. But by far the most publicized and controversial figure in the present debate over suicide is Dr. Jack Kevorkian, who has assisted the terminally ill in taking their lives.

Section One of this compilation deals with the disturbingly high rate of suicide among the young. Gay teenagers, who are prone to harsh rejection from within and outside the home, are even more at risk than the rest of the teen population. Another article in this section concerns the rock star Kurt Cobain, who committed suicide in 1994, and whose songs captured the bleak, frustrated mood of the young adults of the "Generation X."

The Nancy Cruzan case is the focus of Section Two. It raises a number of questions concerning the right-to-die movement, such as under what conditions may the family of a comatose patient have life-support removed? Are advance directives and living wills viable options for those who want to plan in the event they are unable to make life and death decisions? And should individuals have the right to designate a health-care proxy or give someone power of attorney over their health care?

Sections Three and Four are devoted to Dr. Kevorkian. Section Three begins with an account of Derek Humphry, founder of the Hemlock Society, which at first advocated "passive" euthanasia but later disseminated instructions for committing suicide. By the time Humphry's *Final Exit,* a manual for ending one's life was published in 1991, Dr. Kevorkian had stepped into the national spotlight. His assisted suicides using a machine called a mercitron, which patients themselves activated, resulted in repeated arrests and court appearances. At the same time, several states, such as California, Washington, and Oregon, launched initiatives to legalize physician-assisted suicides. The debate has pitted church groups and conservatives against humanists and pro-choice advocates.

The editor is indebted to the authors and publishers who have granted permission to reprint the material in this compilation. Special thanks are due to Joyce Cook and the Fulton (N.Y.) Public Library staff, and to the staff of Penfield Library, State University of New York at Oswego.

ROBERT EMMET LONG

February 1995

I. ADOLESCENT AND YOUNG ADULT SUICIDE

EDITOR'S INTRODUCTION

Suicide has recently risen sharply among the young. Section One explores this phenomenon, and the stresses particular to members of this group. The pressure to succeed is discussed by Brian O'Reilly in an article from *Fortune* on the difficulty some successful business executives have in parenting, and the effect it has on their children. O'Reilly points out that some teenagers attempt to escape anxiety with drugs, alcohol, and suicide, which is the second-leading cause of death among 15- to 19-year-olds after accidents.

According to one report, approximately 40 percent of high school students have contemplated suicide. Those who followed through, however, suffered from an unusual compulsion or were especially vulnerable, such as drug or alcohol abusers, the learning disabled, and victims of sexual abuse. Nancy Wartik's article from *American Health* chronicles the suicide of 19-year-old Jerry Cohen, followed by an overview of teenagers who take their lives, and steps, such as suicide prevention classes, that can be taken to combat this growing problem. Next, Ritch C. Savin-Williams, in the *Journal of Consulting and Clinical Psychology,* discusses the suicide rate of gay adolescents, which is triple that of others in the same age group.

In the last article, from *Rolling Stone,* Anthony DeCurtis analyzes the death of Kurt Cobain, the rock star who took his life in April 1994 at the age of 27, and whose music came to voice the disillusion of his peers, the "Generation X," young people alienated by the lack of values they perceive in present society.

WHY GRADE 'A' EXECS GET AN 'F' AS PARENTS[1]

You can solve that thorny problem in Jakarta with a few crisp commands to your underlings, but ask your teenage son why he got in late last night and you're reduced to impotent fury in seconds. For all their brains and competence, powerful, successful executives and professionals often have more trouble raising kids than all but the very poor. Alas, the intensity and single-mindedness that make for corporate achievement are often the opposite of the qualities needed to be an effective parent.

Six years ago when AT&T was in the throes of divesting its operating companies, Ma Bell conducted a survey of its managers and top executives and discovered that their kids caused these employees more stress and worry than anything else, including their careers. Says attorney Robert Weinbaum, head of antitrust and marketing law at General Motors: "I think it's real tough for kids growing up in families where the parents are highly successful." Weinbaum went through years of turmoil with his own son before they resolved their difficulties.

Many parenting problems are common to everyone: paralyzing uncertainties about how strict or lenient to be, a sense of powerlessness in the face of peer pressure, preoccupation with professional problems, or just plain forgetting what a kid needs from mom or dad. But raising happy, successful children is not a hopeless task or just dumb luck. Interviews with scores of educators, psychologists, drug experts, executives, and troubled teens reveal some consistent differences between kids who turn out "good" and those who go "bad," and provide some suggestions on how to avoid the most colossal blunders.

The most important thing a parent can do for a child is to encourage a high sense of self-esteem. Easier said than done, of course. The tricky part is helping children set appropriate, satisfying goals and then providing an environment that lets them reach the goals on their own. Building your child's self-esteem is an inconvenient, time-consuming, and maddeningly imprecise occupation, and don't be amazed if you mess up. Intuition and

[1]Article by Brian O'Reilly, staff writer, from *Fortune* 121:36–39+ Ja 1 '90. Copyright © 1990 by *Fortune*. Reprinted with permission.

good intentions often don't seem to be much help, and you need skills that rival a pilot's ability to land a jet at night on an aircraft carrier. But kids who have a sense of self-worth flourish. Kids who don't are vulnerable to drug and alcohol abuse, unwanted pregnancy, anxiety, depression, and suicide. Even worse, they may not get into Harvard.

In case your long-range plans include working triple time at the office until the brats turn 17, then deftly steering them into the Ivy League, listen up. Serious emotional problems usually start when children are in sixth to eighth grade, and hit crisis proportions by the sophomore year of high school. Says Sheila Ribordy, a clinical psychologist at De Paul University: "By junior year they're on track or in serious trouble."

Don't think your brains, money, or success will pave the way to parenting glory. In a survey of large corporations providing extensive insurance coverage, Medstat Systems, an Ann Arbor, Michigan, health care information firm, discovered that some 36% of the children of executives undergo outpatient treatment for psychiatric or drug abuse problems every year, vs. 15% of the children of nonexecutives in the same companies.

Top executives have special problems as parents. Many are highly educated, driven personalities who routinely put in 12 to 15 hours a day on the job—workaholics, in other words. Says Susan Davies-Bloom, a Connecticut family therapist who treats senior managers: "They are so accustomed to functioning at a high level of control at the office that when they get home, they try to exert the same kind of control."

The milieu that executives attempt to establish at home can be highly stressful for children. The attributes a manager must develop to succeed include perfectionism, impatience, and efficiency. Says Andrée Brooks, author of *Children of Fast Track Parents:* "Contrast those traits with what it takes to meet the needs of a growing child—tolerance, patience, and acceptance of chaos."

During their teens, kids assert their own individuality, rebelling against whatever their parents value most. Unfortunately for the kids of driven executives, what mom and dad often value most is achievement. Says Davies-Bloom: "I find many workaholic executives felt they were mediocre in popularity, grades, and athletics." Frequently the parent tries to create a child who was everything he was not, or thinks he can steer the kid around every pitfall. Sparks fly, and the youngster refuses to perform.

Worse, some parents are so absorbed with their own careers

that they scarcely notice their children, who respond by behaving in increasingly bizarre and dangerous ways to attract attention. "My father worried about me from his desk," says the son of an IBM executive. The kid started stealing from his parents—trinkets, at first. But when he took his father's gun and began disappearing at night, family therapy finally began.

Given 70-hour workweeks, divorce, or a spouse with a career or demanding social schedule, and complications set in fast. You thought buying a big home in a wealthy suburb would bestow bliss on your offspring? Too often it has the opposite effect. Thousands of business people who were No. 1 somewhere else move to towns where everyone else is successful too. All the other kids in school are very bright and also under pressure to achieve.

Soon the parents wonder why their kid isn't at the top of the class. Says Constance McCreery, formerly a public school guidance counselor in Darien, Connecticut: "In wealthy towns you get what I call the Big Apple syndrome. It's the problem of keeping all the children full of enough confidence that they *can* succeed."

Mom and a tightknit community used to be able to keep child rearing running smoothly even if dad was putting in overtime. But most younger mothers work nowadays, and wives of senior executives often have commitments that keep them out of the home, even if they don't have paying jobs. Suzanne Gelber, a benefits consultant, was on the board of a day care center in Chappaqua, New York, where most of the mothers who dropped off their kids did not work. "They have so many philanthropic and social responsibilities that they are very busy women," she says. "They are not home baking brownies."

Nobody can prove that children with nannies wind up in reform school more often than those who don't, but some kid watchers are concerned. Says Tom Collins, executive director of Fairview Deaconess Hospital, an adolescent drug treatment center in Minneapolis: "Every move you make away from kids in pursuit of your own happiness and career increases their chance of getting into trouble. Lending kids out to babysitters and day care makes it a crap shoot."

Ask a bunch of educators how life for well-to-do kids has changed over the years and you get a surprising answer: The children are under far greater strain than their parents ever were to perform well academically and win acceptance to high-prestige colleges. At New Trier Township High School near Chicago, principal Dianna M. Lindsay says, "The pressure to get into a name-brand college is monumental. I see kids buckle under it."

Part of the stress is classic pushy-parent stuff. Says Carol Perry, director of counseling at the exclusive Trinity School in Manhattan: "This is an era of designer children. No parent wants an average child." Adds Lindsay: "Parents want their kids to go to a school whose name is recognized at the country club."

Much of the mounting anxiety springs not from overt parental pressure, however, but from the students themselves, whose values have been not so subtly affected by mom and dad's affluence. Many well-off kids have grown up using a financial yardstick to evaluate themselves and others. But the prospects for these wealthy kids to improve on or at least maintain their current lifestyles are frighteningly slim. "Successful moms and dads come here because the environment breeds success," New Trier's Lindsay observes, "but the kids say, 'I can never match this. This is the best my life will ever be.'"

Students at New Trier are encouraged to do social service, such as working in soup kitchens, and once a year they are asked to fast for a day in recognition of world hunger and donate lunch money to the poor. Says Lindsay: "We have to teach the kids there are other standards besides material possessions. It's a real, serious problem."

The predictable consequences of all the stress on kids: alcohol, drugs, and suicide, the ultimate parental nightmare. Teenage suicide rates doubled between 1968 and 1987, to 16.2 per 100,000 boys and 4.2 per 100,000 girls. Suicide now ranks as the second cause of death, after accidents, among 15- to 19-year-olds. Some factors that prompt suicide, such as depression caused by the death of a loved one, are not the result of demanding parents. But pressure to do well in school and athletics is a contributor to suicide, and children in a close-knit family are less likely to kill themselves than kids without strong family ties.

Though drug use appears to have peaked in the early 1980s, it is still very high. According to the University of Michigan's Institute for Social Research, more than half of all high school seniors have reported using an illicit drug at some time in their lives—usually marijuana—and a third have tried something stronger. Virtually all seniors—92%—have experimented with beer or hard liquor, and in the two weeks before the institute's survey was taken, 35% had been drunk at least once although every state now bans drinking under age 21.

Rare is the parent who cannot recall sneaking more than a few beers in his or her youth, but the prevalence of teenage drinking has many people worried. Donald R. Geddis, the principal at Summit High School in New Jersey, is more concerned about the use of alcohol among his students than he is about any other substance. "Its use is so widespread it outstrips all others," he says.

Drinking is starting early—the average age for that first surreptitious sip is 13—before many children have developed better methods of coping with stress. Youngsters are aping the attitude of adults: "I've had a tough week and I'm entitled to blow off a little steam." Worse, drunk kids are also more likely to experiment with other drugs they would shun while sober.

Since practically every kid drinks and most experiment with drugs, what distinguishes those who tinker with the stuff from those who develop a serious dependency is "the degree of anxiety for which they are seeking surcease," says Virginia Kramer Stein, a clinical psychologist in New Jersey. Although no kid is as supremely self-confident as many try to appear, youngsters who think of themselves as losers or unwanted by their busy parents, or who have trouble making friends, are at a higher risk of abusing alcohol and drugs than other kids.

When they drink or take drugs, many kids feel transformed for the first time from awkward geeks into cool and appealing characters. "Addiction has a lot to do with self-esteem," says Jeri, 16, the daughter of a Minneapolis-area businesswoman. Jeri started drinking at 11; then her sister introduced her to marijuana, which she smoked every day through much of her first year of high school. By the time she was in tenth grade, she was caught selling grass, and sent to a rehabilitation program at Fairview Deaconess.

How do parents reduce the stress on their kids, boost their self-esteem, and keep them off drugs? Says Summit High's Geddis: "If I've learned one thing, it is that the main priority for parents is to help their kids find something that makes them feel good about themselves. That's the greatest deterrent to drugs and alcohol."

An important first step is to ease up on relentless pressure to make the youngster perform well in school. Focus only on grades and you're handing the kid a weapon to punish you with. If the child appears "only average" but is attending one of the toughest high schools in the country, find out where he or she ranks among peers on standardized achievement tests. That will help you know whether a B or C average is reasonable.

Do not greet your children every evening with an ostensibly cheery "How'd you do in school today?" It is a very threatening question and often elicits no more than a mumbled "Okay." Good grades help get you into a top college but don't predict a happy, successful life, says Robert Klitgaard, former faculty head of admissions at Harvard's Kennedy school.

In case you forgot, success in high school is not achieved the same way as success in a corporation. You get ahead in a company by climbing the ladder and paying your dues, concentrating on things you're good at, and delegating or avoiding areas where you are not competent. You may be a whiz at corporate finance in part because the job does not require you to decline French verbs or find the area of an isosceles triangle. But your sophomore does not have the luxury of hiring a Harvard MBA to do her home-work.

Don't ignore the possibility that the apple of your eye simply is not as smart as you are. Children have roughly the same IQ as the average of their parents', but there are plenty of deviations. About 7% of the time, a child will be 15 points higher or lower than the parents' average, and one time in a thousand, a 30-point difference will pop up.

The average college graduate has an IQ of 115 and Ph.D.s typically score 130, according to John E. Hunter, a professor of psychology at Michigan State University. "It doesn't take much of a slip, and the child of parents who struggled to get through college will not be able to make it," he adds. (Of course, there's an equal chance your daughter is justified when she calls you stupid.) Though you may be a genius yourself, if you married a good-looking but dim bulb, you can't expect your progeny to send rockets to Mars. If your kid has been a whiz all along, however, and his grades collapse in high school, emotional or drug problems are the likely culprits—not his IQ.

Spend time with the family. Ordering your secretary to book 50 minutes of "quality time" into your schedule is better than nothing, but quality time has a habit of fitting your routine, not the kids'. Del Yocam, 45, former chief operating officer at Apple, religiously went home for dinner at 7 P.M. at least twice during the week, and avoided business commitments on weekends. "The children have come to expect it," says Yocam. In November he retired from Apple. His devotion to his family didn't hurt his career there, Yocam says, but "it's time to move on to other things."

Hugh McColl, chairman of NCNB, the big Southern regional bank, cut out weekend golf and reduced entertaining at night years ago to have more time with his three children. But he still has some regrets about the time he spent away from home. He was coaching his son's YMCA basketball team in the early 1970s, and a league championship game was looming. Instead McColl went to a banking convention, and the team lost by two points. "My son still blames me," says McColl with a laugh. "He figures if I'd been at the game he would have won."

Robert Butler, a senior engineer at Chevron in San Francisco, is also determined not to let his job overwhelm his family. He schedules time for his children, leaving for the office at dawn on days he has to depart early to coach his son's soccer team. Says he: "You can always put things off for the future, but you can't get back the years with your kids."

Use the time you spend with the children to listen sympathetically to them. That skill is particularly difficult for men to acquire, according to Ronald Levant, a Rutgers University psychologist and author of *Between Father and Child*. "Men are not trained to be empathetic listeners," he says. "We're taught to listen to our opponents to discover their weaknesses." Men see themselves as problem solvers, not as shoulders to cry on.

Thus, the father who comes home and sees that his 15-year-old daughter has just eaten a whole box of Oreos will probably want to warn her about pimples and weight. Resist the urge. Just let her pour her heart out. Don't be hurt or angry if she doesn't respond the first dozen times you try to be understanding. If you've been a clod for the past 15 years, she may be confused or think you're trying to trick her.

You may learn from all that listening that your son really doesn't want to go to Stanford, is the laughingstock of Kenilworth when you force him to practice drop-kicking at the country club, and dreads following your footsteps into the brake shoe business because he can't figure out what a brake shoe *is*. Fight the desire to disown him, and he may confess that he is fabulous at lawn bowling and likely to get a scholarship from East Cowflop University to study French cooking.

Go lawn bowling with him and let him whip up some frog legs Provençale for you. You won't enhance your bragging rights with the board of directors, but you will do wonders for his self-esteem. And you could be pleasantly surprised: You may find that a newly energized youngster has replaced the sullen adolescent of just a few weeks before. "There are no lazy teenagers," says Carol Perry. "More likely they're turned off or depressed."

Some parents conclude that boarding schools can do a better job of teaching and raising their children than mom or dad will. For example, a single parent who has to travel on the job might want the youngster in a stable environment that provides a sense of security for both child and parent. Such places range from exclusive prep schools such as Groton, Exeter, and Lawrenceville, which rival Ivy League colleges in admission requirements and costs; to less well-known but highly regarded private institutions such as the Webb Schools in Claremont, California, St. Stephen's Episcopal School in Austin, Texas, and Wayland Academy in Beaver Dam, Wisconsin; to military academies like Valley Forge in Pennsylvania that boast of instilling "conservative Christian values" in their charges.

Then there are boarding schools where many of the kids have serious behavioral and emotional problems, among them drug abuse, petty theft, truancy, or depression. Among these academies are Cedu in Running Springs, California, Franklin Academy in Sabbatus, Maine, and the Brown Schools in Texas. Bob Weinbaum, the GM attorney, sent his son John to the DeSisto School, a prep school in Stockbridge, Massachusetts. With the Broadway producer Joseph Papp among the first board members, Mike DeSisto, a rumpled Catholic ex-seminarian who once ran a private school on Long Island, started the school in 1978. The annual tuition of $19,000 is more than the cost of a year at Yale.

In addition to a rigorous academic schedule, DeSisto students undergo multiple private and group therapy sessions each week. But an important part of their development occurs as the kids learn to be accepting of each other and affectionate. Most conversations seem to begin and end with vigorous bear hugs. DeSisto himself is both warm and demanding. He lets kids pile onto his living room sofa and fall asleep on his lap until the 10 P.M. curfew. But kids don't "graduate" until they complete the course requirements, perform well at increasingly difficult and responsible campus jobs from washing dishes to assigning dorm rooms, and demonstrate they can be effective "parents" for newer arrivals.

If you're committed to winning the Dad or Mom of the Year Award, one of the biggest and most common mistakes you can make awaits you: being a wimpy and overprotective parent. Says Gary McKay, co-author of *The Parent's Handbook:* "One of the greatest handicaps a child can suffer is to be raised by a 'good' parent."

These well-meaning types try to do everything for the kids, rushing upstairs five times to wake them for school, exhorting them to eat breakfast faster, and driving them to school when they miss the bus. All this service winds up depriving the kid of self-confidence and independence, says McKay. Far better to be a "responsible" parent. Buy the youngster an alarm clock, explain that breakfast ends at 7:30, and if he misses the bus let him walk to school. Don't scold, don't say, "I told you so," don't debate, don't give in.

Bob Weinbaum fell into a good-parent trap, trying so hard to be a "fair and reasonable" father that he was coming across as overprotective, vague, and indecisive to his son John. "In retrospect, I wish I had remembered that *I* was the father—that *I* was the one in charge," says Weinbaum, whose credits include winning federal approval for the GM-Toyota deal in Fremont, California, and managing his son's baseball team. John grew up with a lot of love and attention, but Weinbaum now admits he tried to do too much for his son, even his homework. "John told me once I was so involved, I made him feel incompetent."

By the time John was a sophomore in high school, their relationship was in tatters, and both parents were worried. "I remember his violent outrages and kicking the door apart," says Weinbaum. "He was in a lot of pain." Schoolwork deteriorated, and the parents began finding marijuana butts on the floor. When the son started going to parties and not coming home at night, Weinbaum was frazzled. An adolescent treatment center in Detroit determined John's problems were not drug-related, so Weinbaum wound up sending John to the DeSisto School. He graduated in three years and is now at a college near Baltimore.

For all three years Weinbaum and his wife attended monthly group support meetings with other DeSisto parents in the Detroit area and gradually learned how to improve relations with John. "He is a spectacular, wonderful son," says Weinbaum today.

If you plan to run out and start putting your foot down, do not mistake harshness or violence for firmness. Says one tall 17-year-old student at DeSisto: "My father used to throw me up against a wall, demanding that I get better grades. But there was never any follow-through." The boy wanted his parents to talk to him about why he was having trouble in school and offer some help, but they did not. Says he: "Parents often think if they've yelled and sent you to your room that their job is done."

Since so much experimentation with drugs and alcohol begins in the preteen years, start long before they're in sixth or seventh grade to communicate with your children, and practice being assertive. Says Bruce Thompson, superintendent of the middle school in Woodside, a San Francisco suburb: "This is the best time to catch them. They're still little kids, on the way to adults."

How strict is strict enough when dealing with kids on the verge of becoming teenagers? "You ask kids where they're going when they go out," says Thompson. "They do their homework and you check their homework. They show up for dinner, they don't go out on school nights, and when they say they're sleeping over at Johnny's, you call up Johnny's parents and ask if they will be home that evening. Will the child complain? Yes."

When kids in middle school and high school do go out at night, parents should be up and awake to greet them when they return. Says Tom Collins, head of Fairview Deaconess, the drug rehab center in Minneapolis: "Sit down and talk with your kids when they come in. You should be able to say to them, 'You look weird. Have you been doing drugs?'"

If you take time to observe a teen, you can soon tell whether he's drunk or stoned. Do kids want to be stopped? Absolutely. "If you don't see it soon enough," Collins warns, "your child will go through lying, stealing, cheating. It gets rolling and you can't stop it until the kid is in so much pain he wants treatment."

Many parents don't even suspect a problem until they find drugs or get a call from police or school officials. Warning signs that a kid is becoming an abuser include suddenly erratic grades, skipping school, dropping out of extracurricular activities, avoiding the family, swings in mood, violence, depression, no savings from a part-time job, and a crop of unfamiliar and unimpressive new friends.

Most parents will never have to deal with anything more serious than their own chronic sense of clumsiness and frustration. In case you think you are hopelessly inept and suspect your kids secretly fired you a long time ago, be assured that you are far more influential than you suspect. "The best manipulation parents have is their attention. It is an extraordinary power that most of them neglect to use," says David, 17, the troubled son of a high-ranking Ford executive. "Parents are very important to kids—more than they will ever let on."

JERRY'S CHOICE: WHY ARE OUR CHILDREN KILLING THEMSELVES?[2]

"I sit alone, sad and quiet, contemplating death. My hopes and dreams have turned to dust; inside my soul, emptiness. I look back on the bright, bubbly, always contented child that I was, every day and everything was just so great, nothing could really go wrong. Even as I sit and contemplate the end of my life by my own hand, I'm so empty I can't even cry."

JERRY COHEN, 19

A slender college sophomore with curly blond hair and direct green eyes, Jerry Cohen was finding the journey to adulthood a rough one. In high school he'd been an honors student, an easy-going kid who liked to go on class trips and was on the swim team, but now he was close to flunking out of his midwestern college and he had been kicked out of his fraternity after a quarrel with other members. Things were going so badly he left school for a while, and it was then, on a fall day in 1988, that he said something to his mother she's been turning over in her mind ever since. They were in the car, not far from the family home in suburban New Jersey.

"We passed Child World," Barbara Cohen recalls, "and grown up as he was, Jerry pointed to Child World and said, 'Mom, that's really where I want to go.'

"I said, 'What are you talking about?'

"He said, 'I just want to play with toys the rest of my life.'"

With the new year Jerry returned to school, but by spring break he came home so glum his parents sent him to a therapist. His father Jon also took him aside and asked if he'd ever thought of "hurting himself."

Jerry laughed. "Come on, Dad," he said. "I wouldn't even know how."

One night a few weeks after Jerry returned to college, the

[2]Article by Nancy Wartik, writer on health and psychology, from *American Health* 10:73–76 O '91. Copyright © 1991 by *American Health*. Reprinted with permission.

Cohens were told by their local police station to contact the dean of students. But the dean wasn't in, and Jerry wasn't answering his line either. So Barbara and Jon Cohen, panic rising in them like fever, sat trying to watch *L.A. Law.*

Finally the phone rang. "I have terrible news," the dean said. "Your son hanged himself this afternoon in his dorm room."

The trees were in fresh new leaf when Jerry Cohen was buried in jeans and a Grateful Dead T-shirt. He left a long note, explaining his decision with astonishing detachment, and he also left behind, as all youths who kill themselves do, a haunting question: why?

His best friend at college, Randi, says simply of the choice Jerry made: "Too loving a person, too harsh a world."

More and more young Americans have been choosing to take their own lives. About 5,000 people 24 and under killed themselves in 1988. The real toll may be twice as high, since some families conceal a child's suicide, and the true motive for a number of fatal accidents does not always come to light. In the last 30 years, the rate of reported suicides among young people has nearly tripled. After accidents (mostly auto), suicide is the leading cause of death among 15- to 19-year-olds.

Every suicide concludes a unique and complex story, but statistics about the young people who commit it yield a few generalizations: It is five times as common among young men as women; the rate for whites is more than double that for blacks; youth rates are highest in the western states; and Ivy Leaguers are more likely to take their lives than other university students.

Although there are many theories to explain the youth suicide "epidemic," as some researchers call it, no consensus has been reached. Some experts see it as a symptom of the nation's moral and religious decay or the breakdown of the family. Others blame the ease with which young people obtain access to alcohol, drugs and guns. Another theory is that suicide rates are higher in more "crowded" generations when kids are under more pressure because of increased competition to succeed. And a few critics charge that the media, hungry for lurid headlines, have blown what is really a minor problem way out of proportion.

In any event, schools across the country now teach the unlikely subject of suicide prevention. Psychologists, meanwhile, are trying to understand which types of kids most commonly take their lives. "Research is showing remarkably specific characteristics in young people who commit suicide," says Dr. David Shaffer, a child psychiatrist at the New York State Psychiatric Institute in New York City. "We need to identify high-risk kids and give them the best possible treatment. Suicide is never inevitable."

"I still don't believe it," Barbara Cohen says. "This kid has me so baffled. How could he have chosen this? He couldn't have been in his right mind. Why he wasn't—that's what drives me crazy. I guess I'll never really know."

By all outward appearances, Barbara and Jon, both in their late forties, lead normal lives. She's a sales rep and he's an accountant. But like detectives in a mystery where the key character has removed the most vital clues from the scene, they're still groping for answers, trying to understand what brought the older of their two children to his final, terrible decision. "Of all the things I thought I'd have to face in my life, this was not one of them," Jon says. "I always thought there was a purpose for everything, it was all part of a master scheme. But I will never find an explanation for this."

The Cohens knew Jerry started smoking marijuana in high school, but as children of the '60s they weren't particularly concerned. Only after Jerry's death did they learn he'd also taken LSD, about a hundred times. A week before he hanged himself, he took so many drugs at a Grateful Dead concert that he passed out and hit his head. Friends feared he'd sustained a concussion, but he refused to see a doctor.

It was like Jerry to deny that anything was really wrong. Looking back, his cousin Linda recalls a poem he showed her a year before he died. It was "very gloomy," she says, "all about death and emptiness. I asked Jerry, 'Are you feeling this?'

"He said, 'No, it's just something I wrote down.'

"That was how it went," she continues. "He'd show you something, say something, then wouldn't let you touch it. He always said what you wanted to hear."

Every indication is that Jerry spent his last days deeply depressed. He skipped classes, slept a lot, ate little. He told his parents he was seeing a school therapist, but after his death they learned he hadn't sought help.

Three days before he died, during a phone call, Jerry told his brother Mark that he was failing school and thinking of hanging himself. Mark cried; Jerry recanted the threat. Not wanting to alarm his parents, Mark kept it to himself. "If only Mark had been educated to know that when they already have a plan, that's when the red light is supposed to go on, that's when you break the bond of friendship and try to save a person's life," Barbara says. "Of course we don't blame Mark. But maybe if he'd told us, Jerry would be alive today."

In the inverted logic of suicide parlance, many teenagers "fail" for each one who "succeeds." A Gallup poll released last April indicated that at least 6% of the teens surveyed had made an attempt. Though young women are more than three times as likely to attempt self-annihilation as young men, males are so much likelier to accomplish it that the disparity is one of the major puzzles in the field today.

One explanation, researchers say, is that men are more impulsive and violent than women. What's more, men tend to be handier with guns, a particularly unforgiving suicide method. In 1988, seven times as many men as women fatally shot themselves; overall, firearms accounted for 60% of all youth suicides. By contrast, young women who attempt suicide are far likelier to do it with drugs—a method allowing more second chances.

Still, there's more to the sex disparity than guns or machismo. "Why are males using more deadly means?" asks Dr. Carol Huffine, research director at the California School of Professional Psychology in Alameda, Calif. "Because they *want* to kill themselves, and women often don't." One of the critical factors may be society's more rigid expectations for men, she adds. "The pressure to conform is greater, and costs in self-esteem are higher if they don't. It's not terrible if a girl is called a tomboy—women brag about it as adults. But it's *terrible* if a boy is called a sissy."

Dr. Barry Garfinkel, director of the University of Minnesota's child and adolescent psychiatry division, agrees. "The coach is still saying to guys, 'Only sissies cry, don't be a wimp, pull yourself up by your own bootstraps.'" Programs he has developed in Minnesota high schools teach students to relieve stress by opening up. "*The* major preventive we use in schools is saying it's okay to share your feelings, it's not wimpy," says Garfinkel. "Girls can reveal their feelings and talk, get help if they need it. Boys often have trouble even formulating into words what they feel."

Researchers have identified circumstances that seem to put young people under extra pressure to commit suicide. It's estimated three out of four youth suicide victims have abused drugs or alcohol. They are also more likely than other kids to have been sexually abused or to be learning disabled, homosexual or close to someone who committed suicide. Indeed, when the adolescent pressure to conform takes a morbid turn, the rare but intensely publicized outbreaks of "copycat" suicides make a town such as Plano, Tex., or White Plains, N.Y., briefly notorious.

Alcohol, not surprisingly, often lubricates that most fateful decision: It's found in the blood of half of all adolescent victims. Experts also point to the effect of "last straws." Research shows most vulnerable young people kill themselves within hours or days of some calamity—a bad report card, a broken love affair, a nasty fight with parents or a scrape with police.

Yet only a very small percentage of kids in crisis choose death as a way out. This undeniable truth has helped convince many in the field that most youth suicides are an outcome of some form of mental illness. "Ninety out of 100 kids who kill themselves meet a psychiatric diagnosis," says Garfinkel. "Kids don't commit suicide just because they've been harshly treated or life's dealt them a bad hand. It's the internal processing going on, not merely the facts of one's horrible existence." Unfortunately, mental illness isn't always an obvious condition, and adolescent angst is too easily dismissed as "just a phase."

After many years of minimizing the problem, researchers are now beginning to take adolescent mental disorders seriously. Says Dr. Michael Stanley, a professor of psychiatry and pharmacology at Columbia University: "Only recently and reluctantly have health professionals even acknowledged that children get mentally ill. For a long time it wasn't a commonly held belief."

Depression seems to be striking at an earlier age than ever. According to the National Institute of Mental Health (NIMH), the illness is most likely to appear for the first time in 15- to 19-year-olds. Why today's youngsters are more likely than those of previous generations to fall victim to disabling melancholy is still under debate. But one thing is clear: "The more kids who are depressed, the more youth suicides there will be," says Garfinkel.

A cluster of psychological problems known as "conduct disorders" may also play a potent role in youth suicides. Young people with conduct disorders are prone to impulsive behavior, substance abuse and run-ins with authority. They often have hair-trigger tempers. When such youths take their lives, researchers see it as "violence turned inward."

Several provocative studies suggest that altered brain chemistry may be linked both to violent, antisocial behavior and to suicide. In the 1970s Swedish psychiatrist Marie Asberg found that suicidal subjects averaged lower levels of the cerebrospinal chemical 5-HIAA than other individuals. The chemical is a by-product of the brain neurotransmitter serotonin, which is believed to regulate mood and aggression. In fact, a significant number of Asberg's subjects with low 5-HIAA levels later killed themselves.

Since that study was first published, other researchers have found that people with low 5-HIAA levels tend to behave aggressively and impulsively. Researchers speculate that basic brain chemistry may predispose some individuals to suicide. So far, data on 5-HIAA have been confined to adult studies, but Columbia's Stanley is conducting one of the first research projects to look at 5-HIAA levels in suicidal adolescents. "The serotonin data are the most potentially promising development in the suicide prevention field," he says. "At some point down the line we may have biochemical methods for identifying and treating at-risk individuals. But we're a long way from a test that says, 'You're suicidal, you're not.'"

Diane Gorenstein is a counselor and community educator at the Middle Earth Crisis Counseling Center in Bellmore, N.Y. When she holds suicide prevention classes in local schools, she asks how many students have friends who've thought of killing themselves. Two out of three raise their hands. This is roughly in line with what national surveys find: Around 40% of high schoolers have contemplated suicide. Alarming as that statistic seems, it reflects an adolescent mindset that is not wholly irrational; at an age when the burdens of maturity are first being felt, it's perhaps not abnormal to contemplate whether "to be or not to be."

Even so, experts say any evidence that an adolescent is struggling with that question should be cause for concern. "Most kids who commit suicide have talked about it," says Dr. Susan Blumenthal, chief of behavioral medicine at NIMH. "I believe in erring on the side of caution." Dr. Dave Clark, director of the Center for Suicide Research and Prevention at Rush-Presbyterian-St. Luke's Medical Center in Chicago, agrees: "I wish I had a nickel for every time parents, in retrospect, said their child once mentioned suicide—and now wished they could go back."

In addition to talk of killing oneself, the warning signs include plummeting grades, changes in personality or appearance, and altered eating and sleeping habits. Suicide prevention classes, once unheard of, now reach about 40% of teens. A few states mandate them. Some are broad-based efforts that teach large numbers of students what to do if they spot the warning signs in themselves or a friend. Alternatively, in "peer helping programs," selected students learn how to recognize a classmate in trouble and to intervene.

In recent years community leaders from scoutmasters to teachers have been trained to prevent suicide. Often they see clues parents don't. But they don't always spot trouble. Consider the recent case of a 14-year-old Long Island, N.Y., boy. Not long after he hanged himself, his mother found essays he'd written for a ninth-grade English class. In one the boy describes going to hell and seeing "tortures unimaginable." "I finally realize I've come home," he writes. Another essay is about going to heaven: "All around me people are happy, joyous, having fun. A feeling of nausea enshrouds me." A third says: "I am the kind of person who yearns for death." The fact that the boy's English teacher was probably the only person to see these disturbing essays and never mentioned their content to anyone still fills the boy's mother with bitterness and sorrow.

Though schools are increasingly tackling youth suicide, their efforts spark controversy among researchers in the field. Last winter the New York State Psychiatric Institute's Shaffer argued in the *Journal of the American Medical Association* that by dwelling on the subject of suicide, many prevention programs can stir up dangerous feelings in vulnerable students—and thus may prompt precisely what they're supposed to prevent. In a survey of hundreds of ninth- and 10th-graders before and after they attended a month-long prevention program, Shaffer found that kids at the highest risk of suicide didn't change their views. "Most teenagers already see suicidal behavior as unusual and dangerous," he says. "They don't need a class to persuade them. Most of these programs try to dramatize suicide, and we worried that in a minority of kids that could even stimulate thoughts of it." He criticizes broad-based programs as a waste of resources and advocates instead that kids most likely to commit suicide get special, intensive treatment.

Shaffer's against-the-grain opinions have angered many health professionals. Gorenstein, for one, points out that the programs Shaffer studied were run by regular teachers, not trained counselors. Moreover, she says, Shaffer missed the point: Programs such as Gorenstein's are meant not only to talk students out of killing themselves but also to teach them how to save a peer's life.

Clearly, no prevention program can be 100% effective. Last winter at one New York City school with a program in place, a student began giving away mementos to his friends—a classic warning sign—and then killed himself a few days later. No one reported his behavior.

Sometimes, though, students do act on what they've learned. Ellen, 18, was in a peer helping program in a New York City high school and "turned in" a friend, a 17-year-old girl she worked with at a restaurant. The girl had quarreled with her family and was virtually living in her car. One day she showed Ellen some small, fresh-cut slashes on her wrists. "You hear of things like this," Ellen says, "but when the time comes, you don't know what to do. It took me a couple of days to realize I should tell the psychologist at my school. We'd learned you *must* turn in someone on a suicide attempt. I knew only the girl's first name and where she went to school. But we called and tracked her down. They got her out of class. Because of what I did, she moved back in with her family. Then the next time I saw her she said, 'Someone turned me in.'

"I said, 'Hey, sorry if I cared about you.'"

While the experts debate the best ways to prevent youth suicide, few would dispute that *something* needs to be done. Various surveys reveal that around 20% of high schoolers are deeply unhappy or have authentic psychiatric problems. And yet, of those, only one in five will see a counselor or therapist. Even after a suicide attempt, few kids see a professional. This is especially troubling because one kid in 10 who fails to commit suicide will someday succeed.

But the task of reducing the woeful number of suicides will require more than just watching over America's youth. Some experts view the problem as an expression of an increasingly self-destructive and violent strain in our national character and argue for a transformation both fundamental and broad. "If our society radically changed its attitudes on alcohol use and gun availability, I think we'd see a decrease in suicide," says Rush-Presbyterian's Clark. "But I doubt we'll do that soon." The Department of Health and Human Services, acknowledging that youth suicide "defies ready solutions," recently declared the problem a public health priority, along with the related issue of conduct disorders.

And Congress has set aside $4 million to study why so many young people, rather than heeding the promise of youth, are choosing to break it.

For Jerry Cohen's parents, the struggle is somehow to find meaning in their loss. These days they're working to set up a prevention program in the local school. Barbara belongs to a self-help group for those who've lost a loved one to suicide; as in hundreds of such groups nationwide, its grieving members gather to exorcise the pain and let the healing begin. "I'm doing better," Barbara says. "Human nature is sort of incredible. We do smile again. We even laugh again. We tell jokes, have a good time. I will survive. But nothing will ever be the same." For his part, Jon visits Jerry's grave often. "I don't want to close the gap," he says. "It scares me to think there'll be a time I won't think of him constantly. He was such a big part of my life." Sometimes on long drives he props a picture of Jerry on the dashboard, enjoying the memory of his boy as solace and company on an otherwise lonely ride.

VERBAL AND PHYSICAL ABUSE AS STRESSORS IN THE LIVES OF LESBIAN, GAY MALE, AND BISEXUAL YOUTHS[3]

[Author's note: An earlier version of this article was prepared for the American Psychological Association (APA) Ad Hoc Subcommittee on Lesbian and Gay Youth in Schools.

I thank the APA Ad Hoc Subcommittee members for their comments on a draft of the article and Kenneth M. Cohen for his help with the final version.

Correspondence concerning this article should be addressed to Ritch C. Savin-Williams, Department of Human Development, Cornell University, Ithaca, New York 14853.]

A common theme identified in empirical studies and clinical reports of lesbian, gay male, and bisexual youths is the chronic

[3]Article by Ritch C. Savin-Williams, member of the Department of Human Development, Cornell University. From *Journal of Consulting and Clinical Psychology* 62/2:26–29 '94. Copyright © 1994 by the American Psychological Association. Reprinted with permission.

stress that is created by the verbal and physical abuse they receive from peers and adults. This article reviews the verbal and physical abuse that threatens the well-being and physical survival of lesbian, gay male, and bisexual youths. This response to gay male, lesbian, and bisexual adolescents by significant others in their environment is often associated with several problematic outcomes, including school-related problems, running away from home, conflict with the law, substance abuse, prostitution, and suicide. Although the causal link between these stressors and outcomes has not been scientifically established, there is suggestive evidence that these outcomes are consequences of verbal and physical harassment.

Despite the increasing public visibility of homosexuality and bisexuality in North American culture, the prevailing assumption among clinicians and researchers is that homoerotic attractions and desires are the province solely of adulthood and not of childhood and adolescence. This misunderstanding and the ensuing clinical and empirical silence and neglect are particularly consequential because lesbian, gay male, and bisexual youths are disproportionately at risk for stressors that are injurious to themselves and others. In some cases, the threat for youths is not merely their mental health but their very lives.

A "fact sheet" published by the Center for Population Options (1992) summarized these difficulties.

Lesbian, gay and bisexual adolescents face tremendous challenges to growing up physically and mentally healthy in a culture that is almost uniformly anti-homosexual. Often, these youth face an increased risk of medical and psychosocial problems, caused not by their sexual orientation, but by society's extremely negative reaction to it. Gay, lesbian and bisexual youth face rejection, isolation, verbal harassment and physical violence at home, in school and in religious institutions. Responding to these pressures, many lesbian, gay and bisexual young people engage in an array of risky behaviors. (p. 1)

In a seminal article, Martin and Hetrick (1988) reviewed the major stressors in the lives of lesbian, gay male, and bisexual youths who sought the services of the Hetrick-Martin Institute (HMI) in New York City. [Author's note: The Hetrick-Martin Institute is a New York City community agency that provides educational and social services to sexual-minority youths ages 12 to 21 years. The Institute, which became a full social service agency in 1983, also help found and staff the Harvey Milk School, a public alternative school for New York City youths.] The lesbian, gay male, and bisexual youths, most of whom are also an ethnic minority in North American culture, often felt discredited and isolated from peers, family members, and religious, educational, and social institutions. Many believed that they must remain hidden and invisible; their lives had to be compartmentalized into the public versus the private. One fear of many youths was that family members and peers would discover their "deviant sexuality" and react in such a way that the youths would be expelled from the home or face violence.

Gay male, lesbian, and bisexual youths experience unique stressors in their lives that are directly related to their sexual behavior and identity. This is evident from early empirical studies of lesbian youths. For example, the major problems reported by 60 gay and bisexual male youths ages 16 to 22 years, were their perceived need to keep their homosexuality a secret and their belief that they were rejected by mainstream society because of their sexual behavior and identity (Roesler & Deisher, 1972). According to Rotheram-Borus, Rosario, and Koopman (1991, p. 191), gay and bisexual youths often feel vulnerable because of "issues of disclosing or being discovered by family or friends, reactions by others to their homosexuality, and chronic stress associated with their homosexuality." Their empirical investigation, conducted with HMI African-American and Hispanic gay and bisexual male youths, reported that the most stressful events the youths faced were "coming out" to others, having their sexual orientation discovered by others, and being ridiculed because of their homosexuality. The youths felt that they had little control over the reactions of others: Would they be rejected or neglected? Ridiculed or assaulted? Raped or sexually abused? The stresses caused by coming out to others and being discovered as gay have been extensively covered in other publications (see review in Savin-Williams & Lenhart, 1990). In the present article, research that addresses verbal and physical abuse and associated outcomes is reviewed, focusing exclusively on investigations conducted with samples of bisexual, lesbian, and gay male youths.

From a traditional scientific perspective, many of these studies are methodologically flawed. They include only a very small number of nonrepresentative lesbian, bisexual, and gay male youths. The vast majority of youths who will eventually identify themselves as lesbian, bisexual, or gay seldom embrace this socially ostracized label during adolescence and thus would never participate in scientific research. Those who do are often in an urban youth-serving agency, come into contact with the legal system, or are members of college campus organizations. At best, the research reported in this article samples a nonrepresentative (e.g., urban, help-seeking, college activists) fraction of an unusual (out to themselves and to others) section of the gay male, bisexual, and lesbian youth population. In addition, measures and procedures in published studies are often not adequately described and the validity and reliability of the instruments are usually unknown. Few studies considered for this review were published in peer-refereed, "rigorous" (i.e., low acceptance rate) journals; most were published as book chapters, conference articles, and invited articles for trade journals. Thus, it is difficult to evaluate their scientific merit. The approach taken in the current review is to include all available data, to note when they converge, and to offer tentative conclusions—fully aware that subsequent research may well present a different perspective on the issues addressed in this review.

Because lesbian, gay male, and bisexual youths who are visible and willing to participate in research studies are often those who are suffering most—physically, psychologically, and socially—clinicians and researchers may unduly present all such youths as weak, vulnerable adolescents who are running away from home, prostituting themselves, abusing drugs, and killing themselves. In actuality, the vast majority of gay male, bisexual, and lesbian youths cope with their daily, chronic stressors to become healthy individuals who make significant contributions to their culture (see Savin-Williams, 1990). This article and the research it highlights must be balanced by research that focuses on the strengths, coping skills, and successes of lesbian, bisexual, and gay male youths.

The majority of empirical research conducted to date addresses the problems faced by gay and bisexual male youths and not those faced by lesbian and bisexual female youths. This literature fundamentally reflects the male bias of scientific research. In addition, research indicates that gay and bisexual male teenagers are more likely than lesbian and bisexual female teenagers to externalize their stress, thus increasing their visibility, and that female teenagers face their sexual identity crises later, after adolescence (see Savin-Williams, 1990). The latter finding suggests that it is more difficult to recruit lesbian than gay male adolescents for research purposes because there are fewer female lesbian and bisexual youths who have identified their sexual identity to themselves and to others. One approach to overcome this deficit would be to use adult lesbians and bisexual women's retrospective reports on growing up attracted to other women. There are, however, questionable assumptions regarding the use of retrospective data for highly charged emotional research issues (Boxer, Cohler, Herdt, & Irvin, 1993). Even if problems of retrospective bias could be overcome, the pace of change in North American culture for lesbian, gay male, and bisexual youths has been so rapid that it is unlikely that the adolescent experiences of adult lesbian and bisexual women are particularly applicable for today's generation of lesbian and bisexual female adolescents. It is for these reasons that this article only reviews data from the lives of lesbian, bisexual, and gay male youths growing up in North America during the past decade (for cross-cultural reports, see Herdt, 1989).

One common theme identified in empirical studies and clinical reports of lesbian, gay male, and bisexual youths is the chronic stress that is often created by peers and family members through their verbal and physical abuse of lesbian, bisexual, and gay male adolescents. In the following sections, the harassment and abuse that threaten gay male, lesbian, or bisexual youth's well-being are reviewed. This response from peers and adults is often associated with several problematic outcomes, such as school-related problems, running away from home, conflict with the law, substance abuse, prostitution, and suicide. The causal link between these stressors and outcomes has not been scientifically established.

Verbal and Physical Abuse and Harassment as Stressors

Significant numbers of lesbian, gay male, and bisexual youths report that they have been verbally and physically assaulted, robbed, raped, or sexually abused by family members and peers (DeStefano, 1988; Martin & Hetrick, 1988; National Gay and Lesbian Task Force, 1982; Remafedi, 1987a, 1987b; Rotheram-Borus et al., 1991). A review of violence inflicted on gay men and lesbians on college campuses revealed that 55% to 72% of those sampled reported verbal or physical abuse (D'Augelli, 1992). The incidence of physical threats of violence reached 25% in several surveys. The most frequent abusers (64%) in D'Augelli's sample of 160 college lesbians and gay men were fellow students and roommates. In 23% of reported incidents, the abusers were faculty, staff, and administrators.

In studies conducted with ethnic-minority youths seeking the services of the HMI, one half reported being ridiculed because of their homosexuality (Rosario, Rotheram-Borus, & Reid, 1992), and 46% had experienced violent physical attacks because of their sexual identity (Hunter & Schaecher, 1990). A survey of the Los Angeles County school system found that the high prevalence of antigay abuse inflicted by classmates was apparently premeditated, rather than a chance occurrence, and that the incidence is escalating dramatically (Peterson, 1989). The most frequent abusers were fellow teenagers. These data correspond with the data collected on antigay violence occurring on college campuses (D'Augelli, 1992).

Peer Harassment

Several studies of lesbian, gay male, and bisexual youths have documented the importance of peers in their lives. For example, among 61 gay and bisexual male college students, 57% reported that the most important person in their life was a gay or lesbian friend (D'Augelli, 1991). By contrast, 15% replied "parents" and 25%, "straight friends." In a study of over 300 lesbian, bisexual, and gay male youths between the ages of 14 and 23 years (Savin-Williams, 1990), youths reported that the most important aspect of their sense of self was having friends of the same sex. For lesbians, relations with parents trailed after female friends, career, academic success, and a love relationship; for gay male youths, relations with parents trailed after all the aforementioned aspects, physical attractiveness, and a social life.

Peer relations can, however, be a source of dissatisfaction and distress. On the basis of intake interviews and records of individual and group counseling of the first 2,000 sexual-minority youths between the ages of 12 and 21 years who either called or visited the HMI, one of the most difficult issues noted by the youths was social isolation (Martin & Hetrick, 1988). Over 95% of the teenagers reported that they frequently felt separated and emotionally isolated from their peers because of their feelings of differentness. Over one half of the gay and bisexual male HMI adolescents had been ridiculed because of their sexuality, usually by peers (Rotheram-Borus et al., 1991). Most abused were youths who failed to incorporate cultural ideals of gender-appropriate behaviors and roles. The rules of socially appropriate behavior and the consequences of nonconformity were known implicitly by most youths.

Other studies support these findings. Thirty percent of Remafedi's (1987b) 29 gay and bisexual male youths were victims of physical assaults, one half of which occurred on school property. Over one half reported regular verbal abuse from classmates, and 40% had lost a friend because of their homosexuality. White male college students in a conservative community feared being verbally and physically harassed; as a result, they were significantly less open about their homosexuality (D'Augelli, 1991). In Sears' (1991) study, 97% of the 36 lesbian, bisexual, and gay male Southern youths recalled negative attitudes by classmates and over one half feared being harassed, especially if they came out in high school. Only two found a peer group that was supportive of lesbian and gay people. Therefore, most passed as heterosexual until graduation.

In D'Augelli's (1992) review, the response to actual harassment or the fear of it among 70% to 80% of the lesbian and gay male college students was to remain hidden. They avoided situations and people that might implicate them as being lesbian or gay. Few (7%) reported the harassment to authorities, and nearly all (94%) expected to be harassed in the future. In a more detailed study, D'Augelli (1991) reported that the primary fear of the gay male college students (mean age, 21 years) was being rejected by parents. Following closely were the fears of being verbally abused and physically harmed because of their sexual orientation. Those less open had more fears, and those who dreaded physical harassment had lower life satisfaction scores.

Adult Harassment

Violence against lesbian, gay male, and bisexual youths often takes place in the home and neighborhood, perpetuated not only by peers but also by adults, including family members. After coming out to their family or being discovered as gay, many youths are "rejected, mistreated, or become the focus of the family's dysfunction" (Gonsiorek, 1988, p. 116). Youths fear retribution more from fathers than from mothers (D'Augelli, 1991). In a study of over 200 lesbian, gay male, and bisexual youths in Chicago (40% White, 30% Black, 12% Hispanic), relations with the mother were significantly better than with the father (Boxer, Cook, & Herdt, 1991). As a result, youths disclosed their sexual orientation earlier and more often to mothers than to fathers (see also Savin-Williams, 1990); many intensely feared their father's reactions to their sexual identity. Indeed, nearly 10% who disclosed to their fathers were kicked out of their home (Boxer et al., 1991).

The harassment may be more harmful than verbal abuse and may lead to physical assaults, including sexual abuse and rape. Martin and Hetrick (1988) found that problems within the family was the second most common presenting complaint of the HMI youths they interviewed, ranging "from feelings of isolation and alienation that result from fear that the family will discover the adolescent's homosexuality, to actual violence and expulsion from the home" (p. 174). Among the HMI lesbian, gay male, and bisexual youths, nearly one half who had suffered violence because of their sexuality reported that it was perpetuated by a family member (Martin & Hetrick, 1988). Others were abused in institutions such as foster homes, detention centers, and churches. Not infrequently, youths blamed themselves because they felt they must have seduced the adult or did not say "no" convincingly enough. In a later survey of 500 HMI youths—primarily male, Black, or Latino and with a mean age of 16.8 years—Hunter (1990) reported that 40% experienced violent physical attacks from adults or peers. Of the gay-related violence, 61% occurred in the family. Data from studies of male prostitutes, runaways, and homeless youths (discussed later) confirm this home-based violence.

Physical violence in the home may also include sexual abuse. The incidence of sexual abuse was 22% in Martin and Hetrick's study (1988). Similar to the pattern found among female heterosexuals, most cases of sexual abuse of lesbian and bisexual female youths occurred in the home. Among the male youths, sexual abuse was also most likely to occur in the home, usually by an uncle or older brother, but sometimes by a father. Two of Remafedi's (1987a) 29 male subjects were victims of incest, one was abused by an older brother and the other by his stepfather and eight uncles. Heterosexually oriented sexual abuse appears to occur more frequently among lesbians than among gay men (Pratch, Boxer, & Herdt, 1991).

Summary

Although definitive data suggesting that bisexual, lesbian, and gay male youths are more frequently ridiculed and abused by peers and family members than are other subpopulations of adolescents are not available, it is clear that these youths face unique harassment because of their sexual behavior and identity. There is sufficient evidence, however, to suggest that the physical and verbal abuse that lesbian, gay male, and bisexual adolescents receive is a source of great stress to them and is detrimental to their mental health.

There are many potential consequences of peer and family harassment. Although research has not yet addressed the sequential, casual pathway between harassment and negative outcomes, the two are clearly associated. In the following section, I discuss some of the negative outcomes that have been associated by researchers and clinicians with the verbal and physical abuse that lesbian, gay male, and bisexual youths experience.

OUTCOMES ASSOCIATED WITH PEER AND ADULT HARASSMENT

School-Related Problems

Many of the school-related problems experienced by lesbian, gay male, and bisexual youths are in response to the verbal and physical abuse that they receive from peers. Forms of violence range from name calling to "gay bashing" (physical attacks). Because much of this violence occurs in schools, school is too punishing and dangerous for many lesbian, gay male, and bisexual youths to tolerate. Hunter and Schaecher (1990) noted that the consequences of peer harassment include poor school performance, truancy, and dropping out of school. These problems have also been noted by counselors in mainstream schools (Price & Telljohann, 1991; Sears, 1988).

Most of the lesbian, gay male, and bisexual students who attended the gay-sensitive Harvey Milk School in New York City had dropped out of other public schools, largely because of peer harassment (Martin & Hetrick, 1988). Over two thirds of the gay and bisexual male youths in another study (Remafedi, 1987a, 1987b) said they had experienced school-related problems: Nearly 40% were truant, and 28% dropped out of school. These problems were manifested in another study, in which 60% of the gay and bisexual male youths failed a grade (Rotheram-Borus et al., 1991).

Rofes (1989), Peterson (1989), Newton and Risch (1981), and Freiberg (1987) pointed out that schools frequently fail to meet the needs of lesbian, gay male, and bisexual youths or stop the harassment because they fear the repercussions, lack the knowledge or resources, or are simply unaware. Many of the teachers and staff may be bisexual, lesbian, or gay but refuse to offer assistance because they fear that they will be accused of recruiting or converting youth.

In an article addressed to school personnel concerning high school students' attitudes toward homosexuality, Price (1982) concluded, "Adolescents can be very cruel to others who are different, who do not conform to the expectations of the peer group (p. 472)." This assessment echoed Norton's earlier view (1976) that the bisexual, lesbian, or gay male adolescent is "the loneliest person . . . in the typical high school of today (p. 376)." Very little has apparently changed in the last decade.

Runaway and Homeless Youths

There is little empirical verification regarding the percentage of runaways who identify themselves as lesbian, gay, or bisexual or the number of lesbian, gay male, and bisexual youths who run away from home. The National Network of Runaway and Youth Services (1991) reported that 6% of all runaways identified themselves as gay or lesbian. Among 12- to 17-year-old African-American and Hispanic male runaways in New York City, 6% considered themselves gay or bisexual (Rotheram-Borus, Meyer-Bahlburg, et al., 1992). According to the U.S. General Accounting Office (1989), 2% to 3% of homeless and runaway youths who sought services or assistance were reported by shelter staff to be lesbian, gay male, and bisexual youths. Another group, street youths who make money from prostitution, were not counted in this 2%-to-3% range. As I note later, many of these youths are likely to be gay male, lesbian, and bisexual teenagers.

These percentages are probably a gross underestimation because few youths are likely to tell authorities and staff their sexual identity. Indeed, investigations of runaways in specific locales have revealed that a much larger percentage of runaway and homeless youths are gay, lesbian, or bisexual (Robertson, 1989; Yates, MacKenzie, Pennbridge, & Cohen, 1988). For example, 40% of street youths in Seattle (Orion Center, 1986) and 30% of the runaway youths in Los Angeles (Peterson, 1989, cited in Kruks, 1991) identified themselves as lesbian, bisexual, or gay.

When the directionality of the question is reversed and these youths are asked if they have ever run away from home, the percentages are considerably higher. For example, nearly one half of bisexual and gay male youths in one study (Remafedi,

1987a) had run away at least once; many, repeatedly. Many of the youths seeking the assistance of the Los Angeles Gay and Lesbian Community Services Center are runaways and throwaways (youths thrown out of the home by parents) who have had arguments and fights with their parents (Brownworth, 1992). Nearly one quarter are HIV-positive. These are vulnerable youths who frequently have good reason to run.

> If you leave home because you've been kicked out for being gay or because you can't cope with the homophobia of your surroundings and you go to a totally different city, you are alone, isolated, on the streets, and very, very vulnerable. (Kruks, as cited in Brownworth, 1992, p. 41)

By leaving, they avoid abuse and maintain the family secret (Burnison, 1986), but they also face a world that is prepared to exploit them.

If these youths do not find programs that meet their needs within 1 or 2 weeks of their arrival on the street, drugs, prostitution, pregnancy, criminal activity, and HIV will take them (Coleman, 1989; Peterson, 1989; Rotheram-Borus et al., 1991). For example, the National Coalition for the Homeless (1990) estimated that 12% to 20% of all homeless youths are HIV-positive. Runaway youths are at very high risk because of the "overwhelming concerns about day-to-day survival [that] can overshadow interest in illness prevention" (Remafedi, 1988, p. 141).

Conflict With the Law and Substance Abuse

Research indicates that gay male, lesbian, and bisexual youths are at high risk for conflict with the law and abusing substances. One quarter to one half of gay and bisexual male youths encounter trouble with the law, largely because of substance abuse, prostitution, truancy, and running away (Remafedi, 1987a; Rotheram-Borus et al., 1991). In the latter study, 23% encountered trouble with the police and 14% had been jailed. Rosario, Hunter, and Rotheram-Borus (1992) found that the male youths they interviewed reported an average of three conduct problems out of 13 listed in the *Diagnostic and Statistical Manual of Mental Disorders* (3rd ed., rev.; *DSM-III-R;* American Psychiatric Association, 1987), sufficient for a diagnosis of conduct disorder. Ninety-two percent of their sample had participated in at least one of the 13 behaviors; this prevalence rate was considerably higher than for comparable surveys of other ethnic-minority youth.

Remafedi (1987a) reported that most of the bisexual and gay

male youths he questioned had used illegal drugs, especially alcohol and marijuana; tobacco and nitrate inhalants were used by almost one half of the youths. Nearly 60% were currently abusing substances and met psychiatric criteria for substance abuse. Seventeen percent had been in a chemical dependency treatment program.

These data correspond to the number of ethnic-minority lesbian, gay male, and bisexual youths who had a drug or alcohol problem in New York City (Rosario, Hunter, et al., 1992; Rotheram-Borus et al., 1991; Rotheram-Borus, Rosario, et al., 1992). In a sample of 20 lesbians, mean age of 19 years, all had consumed alcohol and three quarters had used drugs, including 28% who reported cocaine or crack use (Rosario, Rotheram-Borus, et al., 1992). In a sample of 136 HMI gay and bisexual male youths, 77% drank alcohol, 42% smoked marijuana, 25% used cocaine or crack, and 15% took hallucinogens during their lifetime (Rotheram-Borus, Rosario, et al., 1992). The authors noted that substance use was considerably higher for their sample than among national surveys (e.g., National Institute on Drug Abuse, 1991): ". . . the lifetime prevalence rates for our youths are 50% higher for alcohol, three times higher for marijuana and eight times higher for cocaine/crack" (p. 17). This increased substance abuse may be indicative of the high stress that lesbian, bisexual, and gay male youths experience because of their sexual orientation. It may also reflect the reality that for many youths, of both sexes, the bar subculture, with its emphasis on alcohol, has been a main entry into adult lesbian and gay male communities.

Although there is little documentation regarding the reasons bisexual, lesbian, and gay male youths use illegal substances and engage in criminal activity, they abuse drugs and commit crimes for many of the same reasons as do heterosexual youths (e.g., peer pressure and hedonism), as well as for reasons specific to their sexual identity. The latter include attempts to fog an increasing awareness that they are not heterosexual, to defend against the painful realization that being lesbian or gay means a difficult life lies ahead, and to take revenge against parents and society for rejecting them (Hammond, 1986).

Prostitution

Coleman's review (1989) of the empirical and clinical literature on prostitution among male adolescents revealed that the vast majority (at least two thirds) of male prostitutes are gay or bisexual. Some boys are situational prostitutes, and others make a living from prostitution. The professional "call" and "kept" boys frequently work gay male urban areas; they are the most gay-identified, usually with a well-integrated sense of their sexual identity. These youths are often from a middle-class background and are sufficiently physically attractive to support their prostitution business. Below them in status are "street hustlers," "bar boys," and "prison punks" who frequently come from lower socioeconomic backgrounds and are conflicted about their sexual identification.

According to Coleman, many of these boys begin prostituting in their early teenage years. They drop out of school, use drugs and alcohol, and run away from home or are thrown out by the family because of their sexual orientation. Many of their parents are heavy alcohol and drug users. Consistent with their family pattern, 20% to 40% of prostitutes also abuse drugs (including heroin) and alcohol. They run away from home to escape a family situation that is frequently chaotic and where they feel misunderstood, unwanted, and rejected. Over one half said they had been physically abused or raped. At some point in their lives most said they had been coerced into having unwanted sex. One half had been treated for at least one sexually transmitted disease and most were at high risk for HIV infection.

Those who become street hustlers face a difficult life. In Minneapolis, 75% of male street hustler youths are gay, with a history of dropping out of school, substance abuse, homelessness, and running away from home (Freiberg, 1985). They view themselves as "sluts and whores," have low self-esteem, and want to quit hustling but see no other option. In desperate need of money, they feel that they have no choice except to mug others or prostitute themselves. Most left home because they were thrown out by their parents, but they did not thereby escape sexual abuse, violence, and drugs. Among HMI gay and bisexual male youths in New York City, 23% had exchanged money or drugs for sex at some point in their lives (Rotheram-Borus, Rosario, et al., 1992).

Many male street hustlers are victims of rape and exploitation (Groth & Birnbaum, 1979). They face the trauma of male-male rape and the difficulties that gay male youths have in being taken seriously in reporting the crime and garnering support from authorities. They often have feelings of being "less of a man" and experience physical, emotional, and psychological problems.

Davis and Leitenberg (1987) concluded in their review of adolescent sex offenders that there is little information when the victim of rape is male.

Data on adolescent female-female rape and young lesbian prostitution are difficult to find, although it is clear that, like many heterosexual women, young lesbians have been sexually abused and raped by men (Rothblum, 1990). Rosario, Rotheram-Borus, et al. (1992) reported that 5 of 20 Hispanic and Black New York City lesbian adolescents had exchanged sex for drugs or money. The rate of prostitution among other samples of lesbian adolescents is unknown.

Many youths report that they became prostitutes to survive and to escape physical, sexual, and emotional abuse in their homes and schools. The money helped them become independent from their families; for some, prostitution was a source of excitement and adventure in an otherwise dreary life. On closer examination, it is also clear that many youths turned to prostitution to meet nonsexual needs, such as to be taken care of, to receive affection, and for others to help them cope with their homosexuality. Among their fellow prostitutes, they found camaraderie and kinship that substituted for the neglect or rejection they received from their biological families and peers.

Suicide

Suicide among bisexual, gay male, and lesbian youths has received considerable attention during the last several years. A controversy emerged after the publication of the "Report of the Secretary's Task Force on Youth Suicide" and its quick repudiation by the administration of George Bush in response to conservative and religious opposition. According to the report, suicide is the leading cause of death among lesbian, gay male, and bisexual youths, primarily because of the debilitating effects of growing up in a homophobic society. They are two to three times more likely to kill themselves than are heterosexual youths. In fact, they constitute 30% of all adolescent suicides. The author of the report (Gibson, 1989, pp. 3–110) suggested that one of the primary culprits "is a society that discriminates against and stigmatizes homosexuals while failing to recognize that a substantial number of its youth has a gay or lesbian orientation."

The empirical documentation is of one accord: The rate of suicide among gay male, bisexual, and lesbian youths is considerably higher than it is for heterosexual youth. Studies of lesbian, gay male, and bisexual youths report suicide attempts in the 20% to 40% range (Remafedi, 1987a; Remafedi, Farrow, & Deisher, 1991; Roesler & Deisher, 1972; Rotheram-Borus, Hunter, & Rosario, 1992; Schneider, Farberow, & Kruks, 1989). These rates increase for special populations of gay male, bisexual, and lesbian youths: 41% of the girls and 34% of the boys who report being violently assaulted (Hunter, 1990); 53% among homeless and street youths (Kruks, 1991); 41% of those seeking assistance at service agencies (National Gay and Lesbian Task Force, 1982); and adolescents particularly sensitive to feeling rejected by others (Schneider et al., 1989).

Remafedi et al. (1991) studied 137 gay and bisexual male adolescents, ages 14 to 21 years. Most (82%) are White, volunteered for the research project, and resided in Minnesota or Washington. One third had at least one intentional self-destructive act; one half of these youths had multiple attempts. Remafedi et al. noted that, "the gravity of some attempts is reflected in the rate of subsequent hospitalization (21%), the lethality of methods (54%, moderate to high risk), and the victims' inaccessibility to rescue (62%, moderate to least rescuable) (p. 873)." The suicide attempts were frequently linked with sexual milestones, such as self-identification as gay or coming out to others. The most cited reason for attempting suicide was family problems. Summarizing their psychosocial data predicting suicide attempts, Remafedi et al. concluded that "compared with non-attempters, attempters had more feminine gender roles and adopted a bisexual or homosexual identity at younger ages. Attempters were more likely than peers to report sexual abuse, drug abuse, and arrests for misconduct (p. 869)." Unlike previous studies, suicide attempts were not related to running away from home, depression, hopelessness, suicidal ideation, violence, discrimination, or loss of friendship. The attempters came from dysfunctional families, used drugs (85% reported illicit drug use), and acted out in other antisocial behaviors (more than one half had been arrested).

A study of 108 gay college men, primarily White (70%) and Latino (15%) and ranging in age from 16 to 24 years, in Los Angeles was undertaken by Schneider et al. (1989). Over one half of the youths reported that they occasionally had suicidal thoughts, considered suicidal action, formed a suicide plan, or made a suicide attempt. This group was characterized as having

alcoholism in the family, physical abuse from family members, no
religious affiliation, and a perception that those who usually supported them rejected their homosexuality. Twenty percent of the
total sample reported that they made at least one suicide attempt;
9% made multiple attempts (2 to 14 times). The youngest attempt
was at age 12, and one half of the youths received no treatment
after their first attempt. At the time of first attempt, the youths
felt hopeless, worthless, alienated, lonely, and helpless. Compared
with nonsuicidal gay male youths, attempters were significantly
younger when they first became aware of their homoerotic attractions (8 versus 11 years), first labeled their feelings but not themselves as homosexual (12 versus 14 years), and first became involved in a same-sex romantic relationship (16 versus 18 years).
Although most attempters were aware of their same-sex attractions before their first suicide attempt, few had reached the point
of identifying themselves as gay, felt positive about their sexual
orientation, or had told others about their sexual identity. Attempts were most likely to occur when an individual was question-
ing his heterosexual identity or after same-sex sexual activities.
Schneider et al. concluded that "suicidal behavior in gay youths
may be the product both of familial factors that predispose
youths to suicidal behavior, and of social and intrapersonal
stressors involved in coming to terms with an emerging homosexual identity" (p. 381).

A group of younger (aged 14 to 19 years) and more ethnically
diverse gay and bisexual male youths (47% Hispanic, 28% Black,
11% White, 14% other) from New York City were studied by
Rotheram-Borus, Hunter, et al. (1992). Thirty-nine percent had
attempted suicide; of these, 52% made multiple attempts. An
additional 37% of the 139 youths thought about suicide every day
for at least 1 week, and 49% said they had a family member or
friend who had attempted or completed suicide. Nearly 60% reported suicidal ideation during the week before data collection.
The attempters did not differ from the nonattempters in stressful
life events, but they experienced more gay-related stressors, including coming out to parents (53% versus 30%), being discovered as gay by parents (37% versus 23%) or other family members
(41% versus 28%), and being ridiculed for their sexual identity
(57% versus 45%).

Psychiatrists who specialize in therapy with adolescent patients have speculated that the most frequent causes of suicide
among lesbian, bisexual, and gay male adolescents are feelings of

disenfranchisement, social isolation, rejection from family or peers, and self-revulsion (Kourany, 1987). The high risk among lesbian, bisexual, and gay male youths to suicidal ideation, attempts, and completions has been brought to the attention of psychiatrists (Kourany, 1987), social workers (Hunter & Schaecher, 1987), health educators (Remafedi, 1985), and therapists (Coleman & Remafedi, 1989; Rothblum, 1990). Unfortunately and tragically, few have listened.

Conclusion

Youths who are known to be lesbian, gay, or bisexual receive considerable verbal and physical abuse from peers and, all too frequently, from parents and other adults. These threats of physical harm and verbal abuse that bisexual, lesbian, and gay male youths are subjected to are sources of great stress to them, are detrimental to their mental health, and often correlate with negative outcomes such as school-related problems, substance abuse, criminal activity, prostitution, running away from home, and suicide.

Social science research does not allow us to generalize these findings to all bisexual, gay male, and lesbian youths, primarily because most of these youths are not "out" to themselves or to others. Thus, the youths studied to date are not a representative subset of the gay male, bisexual, and lesbian youth population—as noted by Rotheram-Borus, Rosario, et al. (1992): "These youths are atypical in that they have publicly disclosed their sexual preferences by seeking services at a social service agency serving homosexual youths . . ." (p. 15). They may also be "unusual" because those most abused are frequently youths who are "cross-gendered"; they do not or cannot abide by cultural definitions of acceptable feminine and masculine behavior and, thus, do not meet cultural ideals of gender-appropriate behaviors and roles. Deviating from acceptable sex roles is particularly problematic during adolescence.

Males experience intense peer pressure to be "tough" and "macho," and females to be passive and compliant. Although social sex roles are not intrinsically related to sexual orientation, the distinction is poorly understood by most adolescents, as well as by most adults. Adolescents are frequently intolerant of differentness in others and may castigate or ostracize peers, particularly if the perceived differentness is in the arena of sexuality or sex roles. (Gonsiorek, 1988, p. 116)

Peer rejection may not be expressed directly, but it is recognized nevertheless by affected youths.

Although social science research has not addressed the casual pathway between harassment and negative outcomes, the two are clearly associated with each other. Rosario, Hunter, et al. (1992) most explicitly explored the linkages among emotional distress, conduct problems, alcohol and drug use, and sexual risk acts among gay and bisexual ethnic-minority male youths. In their sample, as might be expected, an increase in conduct problems was associated with increased levels of alcohol and drug usage and emotional distress. However, with an increase in conduct problems came a decrease in reported gay-related stress (negative reactions to coming out to others, being discovered as gay, and ridicule from others), suggesting that they may have desensitized themselves to these stresses by their acting-out behavior. Counter to findings with heterosexual youths, the authors' results did not support a single factor underlying multiple problem behavior; thus, it may not be possible to simply generalize research results from heterosexual to sexual-minority youths. Little is known about "normal" developmental pathways among gay male, lesbian, and bisexual youths and how they are similar and divergent from heterosexual youths (Savin-Williams, 1990). What is known is that the issue of sexual identity status is not a minor, insignificant factor in the lives of adolescents. Rosario, Hunter, et al. (1992) noted, ". . . the experience of being gay or bisexual in our society overwhelms any potential differences in social categories involving age, ethnicity, race, social class or geographical region of the country" (p. 19).

The variety of problematic behaviors described in this review may very well end the lives of many bisexual, lesbian, and gay male youths. Running away from home, engaging in high-risk sexual behavior, prostituting oneself, and abusing substances all place youth at high risk for suicide or being the victim of homicide. Those who survive will face throughout their lives the effects of growing up in a homophobic culture. If their social and interpersonal worlds are replete with verbal abuse and the threat of physical harm, youths in North American culture may find it difficult to totally expunge "internalized homophobia," a term Gonsiorek (1988) used to describe lesbian, gay male, and bisexual individuals' incorporation of biases against homosexuality that are prevalent in the social world. "Symptoms" range from covert forms such as self-doubt to overt self-hatred. The latter case "presents in persons who consciously accuse themselves of being evil, second class, or inferior because of their homosexuality. They may abuse substances or engage in other self-destructive or abusive behaviors" (Gonsiorek, 1988, p. 117).

The effects of peer and family harassment may be more severe for bisexual, lesbian, and gay male youth who are early adolescents or ethnic minorities because they may find it more difficult to recognize and accept their homosexuality than do older and White youths. Early adolescents, according to Remafedi (1987a), face several conflicts that hinder their ability to cope with being lesbian, gay, or bisexual: ". . . emotional and physical immaturity, unfulfilled developmental needs for identification with a peer group, lack of experience, and their dependence upon parents who may be unwilling or unable to provide emotional support around the issue of homosexuality" (p. 336).

Ethnic-minority youths who are gay, lesbian, or bisexual may also be at increased risk for the detrimental effects of homosexually oriented verbal and physical abuse. Savin-Williams and Rodriguez (1993) noted three unique tasks that these youths face: ". . . (a) developing and defining both a strong gay identity and a strong ethnic identity; (b) potential conflicts in allegiance, such as reference group identity within one's gay and ethnic community; and (c) experiencing both homophobia and racism" (p. 94). The Black and Hispanic sexual-minority youths at the Harvey Milk School had many signs of emotional isolation, vulnerability, and depression.

Pervasive loss of pleasure, feelings of sadness, change of appetite, sleep disturbance, slowing of thought, lowered self-esteem with increased self-criticism and self-blame, and strongly expressed feelings of guilt and failure. Again, they repeatedly report they feel they are alone in the world, that no one else is like them, and that they have no one with whom they can confide or talk freely. (Martin & Hetrick, 1988, p. 172)

The dilemma for clinicians and other health care professionals is how best to assist sexual-minority youths. Few youths are willing to seek health care providers because they fear disclosure, humiliation, and discrimination. This may be for good reason: Gonsiorek (1988) noted that, rather than the client's actual problem (e.g., feelings of rejection), his or her sexual orientation may become the focus of treatment for the clinician or agency. Because of their prejudices, staff may allow, or even encourage, discrimination and name calling. Even if they are tolerant, they often lack the knowledge or resources to be of assistance to lesbian, bisexual, and gay male youths.

Guidelines are now available to assist health care providers to overcome these shortcomings (Bergstrom & Cruz, 1983; Kus, 1990; Rofes, 1989; Savin-Williams & Cohen, in press; Savin-Williams & Lenhart, 1990). Clinicians and researchers should support the well-being of gay male, lesbian, and bisexual youths by conducting research, enacting policies, and encouraging behaviors that will help minimize the internalized homophobia, self-destructive behaviors, and homicide of our youths.

REFERENCES

American Psychiatric Association. (1987). *Diagnostic and statistical manual of mental disorders (3rd ed., rev.)*. Washington, DC: Author.

Bergstrom, S., & Cruz, L. (1983). *Counseling lesbian and gay male youth: Their special lives/special needs*. Washington, DC: National Network of Runaway and Youth Services.

Boxer, A. M., Cohler, B. J., Herdt, G., & Irvin, F. (1993). Gay and lesbian youth. In P. H. Tolan & B. J. Cohler (Eds.), *Handbook of clinical research and practice with adolescents* (pp. 249–280). New York: Wiley.

Boxer, A. M., Cook, J. A., & Herdt, G. (1991). Double jeopardy: Identity transitions and parent-child relations among gay and lesbian youth. In K. Pillemer & K. McCartney (Eds.), *Parent-child relations throughout life*. (pp. 59–92). Hillsdale, NJ: Erlbaum.

Brownworth, V. A. (1992, March 24). America's worst-kept secret: AIDS is devastating the nation's teenagers, and gay kids are dying by the thousands. *The Advocate*, pp. 38–46.

Burnison, M. (1986, May). *Runaway youth: Lesbian and gay issues*. Paper presented at the Symposium on Gay and Lesbian Adolescents, Minneapolis, MN.

Center for Population Options. (1992). *Lesbian, gay and bisexual youth: At risk and underserved*. Washington, DC: Author.

Coleman, E. (1989). The development of male prostitution activity among gay and bisexual adolescents. *Journal of Homosexuality, 17*, 131–149.

Coleman, E., & Remafedi, G. (1989). Gay, lesbian, and bisexual adolescents: A critical challenge to counselors. *Journal of Counseling & Development, 68*, 36–40.

D'Augelli, A. R. (1991). Gay men in college: Identity processes and adaptations. *Journal of College Student Development, 32*, 140–146.

D'Augelli, A. R. (1992). Lesbian and gay male undergraduates' experiences of harassment and fear on campus. *Journal of Interpersonal Violence, 7*, 383–395.

Davis, G. E., & Leitenberg, H. (1987). Adolescent sex offenders. *Psychological Bulletin, 101*, 417–427.

DeStefano, A. M. (1988, October 7). New York teens antigay, poll finds. *Newsday*, pp. 7, 21.

Freiberg, P. (1985, November 12). Minneapolis: Help for hustlers. *The Advocate*, pp. 12–13.

Freiberg, P. (1987, September 1). Sex education and the gay issue: What are they teaching about us in the schools? *The Advocate*, pp. 42–49.

Gibson, P. (1989). Gay male and lesbian youth suicide. U.S. Department of Health and Human Services, *Report of the secretary's task force on youth suicide, Vol. 3: Prevention and interventions in youth suicide*. Rockville, MD.

Gonsiorek, J. C. (1988). Mental health issues of gay and lesbian adolescents. *Journal of Adolescent Health Care, 9*, 114–122.

Groth, A. N., & Birnbaum, H. J. (1979). *Men who rape: The psychology of the offender*. New York: Plenum.

Hammond, N. (1986, May). *Chemical abuse in lesbian and gay adolescents*. Paper presented at the Symposium on Gay and Lesbian Adolescents, Minneapolis, MN.

Herdt, G. (Ed.) (1989). *Gay and lesbian youth*. New York: Harrington Park Press.

Hunter, J. (1990). Violence against lesbian and gay male youths. *Journal of Interpersonal Violence, 5*, 295–300.

Hunter, J., & Schaecher, R. (1987). Stresses on lesbian and gay adolescents in schools. *Social Work in Education, 9*, 180–189.

Hunter, J., & Schaecher, R. (1990). Lesbian and gay youth. In M. J. Rotheram-Borus, J. Bradley, & N. Obolensky (Eds.), *Planning to live: Evaluating and treating suicidal teens in community settings* (pp. 297–316). Tulsa: University of Oklahoma Press.

Kourany, R.F.C. (1987). Suicide among homosexual adolescents. *Journal of Homosexuality, 13*, 111–117.

Kruks, G. (1991). Gay and lesbian homeless/street youth: Special issues and concerns. *Journal of Adolescent Health Care, 12*, 515–518.

Kus, R. J. (Ed.) (1990). *Keys to caring: Assisting your gay and lesbian clients*. Boston: Alyson.

Martin, A. D., & Hetrick, E. S. (1988). The stigmatization of the gay and lesbian adolescent. *Journal of Homosexuality, 15*, 163–183.

National Coalition for the Homeless. (1990). *Fighting to live: Homeless people with AIDS*. Washington, DC: Author.

National Gay and Lesbian Task Force (1982). *Gay rights in the United States and Canada*. New York: Author.

National Institute on Drug Abuse. (1991). *National household survey on drug abuse: Population estimates 1990*. Washington, DC: U.S. Government Printing Office.

National Network of Runaway and Youth Services. (1991). *To whom do they belong? Runaway, homeless and other youth in high-risk situations in the 1990s*. Washington, DC: Author.

Newton, D. E., & Risch, S. J. (1981). Homosexuality and education: A review of the issue. *The High School Journal, 64,* 191–202.

Norton, J. L. (1976). The homosexual and counseling. *Personnel and Guidance Journal, 54,* 374–377.

Orion Center. (1986). *Survey of street youth.* Seattle, WA: Author.

Peterson, J. W. (1989, April 11). In harm's way: Gay runaways are in more danger than ever, and gay adults won't help. *The Advocate,* pp. 8–10.

Pratch, L., Boxer, A. M., & Herdt, G. (1991). *First sexual experiences among gay and lesbian youth: Person, age, and context.* Manuscript in preparation.

Price, J. H. (1982). High school students' attitudes toward homosexuality. *Journal of School Health, 52,* 469–474.

Price, J. H., & Telljohann, S. K. (1991). School counselors' perceptions of adolescent homosexuals. *Journal of School Health, 61,* 433–438.

Remafedi, G. J. (1985). Adolescent homosexuality: Issues for pediatricians. *Clinical Pediatrics, 24,* 481–485.

Remafedi, G. (1987a). Adolescent homosexuality: Psychosocial and medical implications. *Pediatrics, 79,* 331–337.

Remafedi, G. (1987b). Male homosexuality: The adolescent's perspective. *Pediatrics, 79,* 326–330.

Remafedi, G. J. (1988). Preventing the sexual transmission of AIDS during adolescence. *Journal of Adolescent Health Care, 9,* 139–143.

Remafedi, G., Farrow, J. A., & Deisher, R. W. (1991). Risk factors for attempted suicide in gay and bisexual youth. *Pediatrics, 87,* 869–875.

Robertson, M. J. (1989). *Homeless youth in Hollywood: Patterns of alcohol use.* Berkeley, CA: Alcohol Research Group.

Roesler, T., & Deisher, R. (1972). Youthful male homosexuality: Homosexual experience and the process of developing homosexual identity in males aged 16 to 22 years. *Journal of the American Medical Association, 219,* 1018–1023.

Rofes, E. (1989). Opening up the classroom closet: Responding to the educational needs of gay and lesbian youth. *Harvard Educational Review, 59,* 444–453.

Rosario, M., Hunter, J., & Rotheram-Borus, M. J. (1992). *HIV risk acts of lesbian adolescents.* Unpublished manuscript, Columbia University.

Rosario, M., Rotheram-Borus, M. J., & Reid, H. (1992). *Personal resources, gay-related stress, and multiple problem behaviors among gay and bisexual male adolescents.* Unpublished manuscript, Columbia University.

Rothblum, E. D. (1990). Depression among lesbians: An invisible and unresearched phenomenon. *Journal of Gay & Lesbian Psychotherapy, 1,* 67–87.

Rotheram-Borus, M. J., Hunter, J., & Rosario, M. (1992). *Suicidal behavior and gay-related stress among gay and bisexual male adolescents.* Unpublished manuscript, Columbia University.

Rotheram-Borus, M. J., Meyer-Bahlburg, H.F.L., Rosario, M., Koopman,

C., Haignere, C. S., Exner, T. M., Matthieu, M., Henderson, R., & Gruen, R. S. (1992). Lifetime sexual behaviors among predominantly minority male runaways and gay/bisexual adolescents in New York City. *AIDS Education and Prevention, Supplement,* 34–42.

Rotheram-Borus, M. J., Rosario, M., & Koopman, C. (1991). Minority youths at high risk: Gay males and runaways. In M. E. Colten & S. Gore (Eds.), *Adolescent stress: Causes and consequences.* (pp. 181–200). New York: Aldine.

Rotheram-Borus, M. J., Rosario, M., Meyer-Bahlburg, H.F.L., Koopman, C., Dopkins, S. C., & Davies, M. (1992). *Sexual and substance use behaviors among homosexual and bisexual male adolescents in New York City.* Unpublished manuscript, Columbia University.

Savin-Williams, R. C. (1990). *Gay and lesbian youths: Expressions of identity.* Washington, DC: Hemisphere.

Savin-Williams, R. C., & Cohen, K. M. (Eds.). (in press). *Developmental and clinical issues among lesbian, gay males, and bisexuals.* Fort Worth: Harcourt Brace.

Savin-Williams, R. C., & Lenhart, R. E. (1990). AIDS prevention among gay and lesbian youth: Psychosocial stress and health care intervention guidelines. In D. G. Ostrow (Ed.), *Behavioral aspects of AIDS and other sexually transmitted diseases* (pp. 75–99). New York: Plenum.

Savin-Williams, R. C., & Rodriguez, R. G. (1993). A developmental, clinical perspective on lesbian, gay male, and bisexual youths. In T. P. Gullotta, G. R. Adams, & R. Montemayor (Eds.), *Adolescent sexuality. Advances in adolescent development, Vol. 5* (pp. 77–101). Newbury Park, CA: Sage.

Schneider, S. G., Farberow, N. L., & Kruks, G. N. (1989). Suicidal behavior in adolescent and young adult gay men. *Suicide and Life-Threatening Behavior, 19,* 381–394.

Sears, J. T. (1988, April). *Attitudes, experiences, and feelings of guidance counselors in working with homosexual students: A report on the quality of school life for Southern gay and lesbian students.* Paper presented at the American Educational Research Association Meeting, New Orleans, LA.

Sears, J. T. (1991). *Growing up gay in the South: Race, gender, and journeys of the spirit.* New York: Harrington Park Press.

U.S. General Accounting Office. (1989). *Homelessness: Homeless and runaway youth receiving services at federally funded shelters.* Washington, DC: Author.

Yates, G., MacKenzie, R., Pennbridge, J., & Cohen, E. (1988). A risk profile comparison of runaway and non-runaway youth. *American Journal of Public Health, 78,* 820–821.

KURT COBAIN
1967–1994[4]

Kurt Cobain never wanted to be the spokesman for a generation, though that doesn't mean much: anybody who did would
never have become one. It's not a role you campaign for. It is
thrusted upon you, and you live with it. Or don't.

People looked to Kurt Cobain because his songs captured
what they felt before they knew they felt it. Even his struggles—
with fame, with drugs, with his identity—caught the generational
drama of our time. Seeing himself since his boyhood as an out-
cast, he was stunned—and confused, and frightened, and re-
pulsed, and truth be told, not entirely disappointed (no one
forms a band to remain anonymous)—to find himself a star. If
Cobain staggered across the stage of rock stardom, seemed more
willing to play the fool than the hero and took drugs more for
relief than pleasure, that was fine with his contemporaries. For
people who came of age amid the greed, the designer-drug indul-
gence and the image-driven celebrity of the '80s, anyone who
could make an easy peace with success was fatally suspect.

Whatever importance Cobain assumed as a symbol, however,
one thing is certain: he and his band Nirvana announced the end
of one rock & roll era and the start of another. In essence, Nirvana transformed the '80s into the '90s.

They didn't do it alone, of course—cultural change is never
that simple. But in 1991, "Smells Like Teen Spirit" proved a defining moment in rock history. A political song that never men-
tions politics, an anthem whose lyrics can't be understood, a
hugely popular hit that denounces commercialism, a collective
shout of alienation, it was "(I Can't Get No) Satisfaction" for a
new time and a new tribe of disaffected youth. It was a giant fuck-
you, an immensely satisfying statement about the inability to be
satisfied.

From that point on, Cobain battled to make sense of his new
circumstances, to find a way to create rock & roll for a mass
audience and still uphold his own version of integrity. The pres-

[4]Article by Anthony DeCurtis, staff writer, from *Rolling Stone* 30 Je 2 '94.
Copyright © 1994 by Straight Arrow Publishers Company, L.P. Reprinted with permission.

sure of that effort deepened the wounds he had borne since
boyhood: the broken home, the bitter resentment of the local
toughs who bullied him, the excruciating stomach pains. He
sought purpose in fatherhood. He wanted to soothe in his daughter, Frances Bean, his own primal fears of abandonment. He
managed, finally, only to perpetuate them.

Cobain's life and music—his passion, his charm, his vision—
can be understood and appreciated. His death leaves a far more
savage legacy, one that will take many years to untangle. His suicide note and Courtney Love's reading of it say it all. In his last
written statement Cobain reels from cracked-actor posturing ("I
haven't felt the excitement . . . for too many years now") to detached self-criticism ("I must be one of those narcissists who only
appreciate things when they're alone") to self-pity ("I'm too sensitive") to a bizarre brand of hostile, self-loathing gratitude
("Thank you all from the pit of my burning, nauseous stomach")
to, of all things, rock-star clichés ("It's better to burn out than to
fade away").

Left with that, Love careens from reverence ("I feel so hon-
ored to be near him") to pained confusion ("I don't know what
happened") to exasperation ("He's such an asshole") to anger
("Well, Kurt, so fucking what? Then don't be a rock star") to
sobbing, heartbreaking guilt ("I'm really sorry, you guys. I don't
know what I could have done").

No answers are forthcoming, because there are none. Suicide
is an unanswerable act. It is said to be the one unforgivable sin,
though our age has sought to forgive it by explaining it away in
psychological or chemical terms. Earlier eras were not so kind.
Suicides were buried at the crossroads. The message was severe:
You were at an impasse in your life and lacked the faith to make
your way through it. Our lives are no easier to bear than yours.
We may fall, but you chose to fall. We will make our way over you
down the road of our destiny.

But suicide sends its own remorseless message. True, it is the
ultimate cry of desperation, more harrowing than any scream
Cobain unleashed in any of Nirvana's songs. True, he was in
agony and saw no other way to end it. But suicide is also an act of
anger, a fierce indictment of the living. If the inability to live is
"sensitive," the ability to live comes to seem crass. "You're so good
at getting over," the final message runs. "Get over this."

At 27 years old, Kurt Cobain wanted to disappear, to erase
himself, to become nothing. That his suicide so utterly lacked

ambivalence is its most terrifying aspect. It all comes down to a stillness at the end of a long chaos: a young man sitting alone in a room, looking out a window onto Lake Washington, getting high, writing his goodbyes, pulling a trigger. You can imagine the silence shattering and then collecting itself, in the way that water breaks for and then envelops a diver, absorbing forever the life of Kurt Cobain.

II. NANCY CRUZAN AND THE "RIGHT TO DIE"

EDITOR'S INTRODUCTION

While Section One focuses on suicide among the young, Section Two deals with the right-to-die movement, which has gathered force over the last decade. If a patient slips into a coma which appears irreversible, can life support systems be removed? Or should the patient be forced to live in this condition indefinitely? What role should physicians and family members be allowed to play in such life and death situations?

In the first article, from *Time,* Nancy Gibbs discusses two publicized right-to-die cases, that of Karen Ann Quinlan and that of Nancy Cruzan. In 1975, after Quinlan had been comatose for seven months, her father petitioned the New Jersey Supreme Court to have her respirator turned off. The court concurred, and after the ruling was put into effect Quinlan lived nine years breathing on her own. The more recent case of Nancy Cruzan, in a coma for seven years, is different. Unlike Quinlan, Cruzan was being kept alive by a feeding tube, which if removed, as her family asked the U.S. Supreme Court, would have led shortly thereafter to her death. Cruzan's case is not rare, for there are 10,000 other patients like her today in the United States.

Writing for *Newsweek,* Katherine Ames reports on alternatives used to control the process of dying. For example, people have increasingly adopted a living will, which outlines the measures to be taken if a life-threatening illness incapacitates them. Another measure is a health-care proxy, which designates a friend or family to act in such a case. Establishing a durable power of attorney for health care endows the designee with even more decision-making power. Furthermore, a new federal law, the Patient Self-Determination Act of 1990, requires a hospital participating in Medicare or Medicaid to ask all adult patients it admits whether they have advance directives, such as a living will.

The third article, by Elisabeth Rosenthal, from *Discover,* reveals how the medical definition of death is open to change, which affects the decision of when to terminate life support systems.

LOVE AND LET DIE[1]

Just as I choose a ship to sail in or a house to live in, so I choose a death for my passage from life.
                                                              —Seneca (4 B.C.–A.D. 65)

Nancy Cruzan, now 32, has done nothing for the past seven years. She has not hugged her mother or gazed out the window or played with her nieces. She has neither laughed nor wept, her parents say, nor spoken a word. Since her car crashed on an icy night, she has lain so still for so long that her hands have curled into claws; nurses wedge napkins under her fingers to prevent the nails from piercing her wrists. "She would hate being like this," says her mother Joyce. "It took a long time to accept she wasn't getting better." If they chose, the Cruzans could slip into Nancy's room some night, disconnect her feeding tube, and face the consequences. But instead they have asked the U.S. Supreme Court for permission to end their daughter's life.

The Cruzan petition not only marks the first time the court has grappled with the agonizing "right-to-die" dilemma; it may well be the most wrenching medical case ever argued before the high bench. To begin with, Nancy is not dying. She could live 30 years just as she is. And since she is awake but unaware, most doctors agree that she is not suffering. But her parents are suffering, for it is they who live with her living death. They are so convinced Nancy would not want to go on this way that they have asked the courts for authorization to remove her feeding tube and "let her go." A lower-court judge gave that permission, but the Missouri Supreme Court, affirming "the sanctity of life," reversed the ruling. Now the U.S. high court must consider whether the federal Constitution's liberty guarantees, and the privacy rights they imply, include a right to be starved to death for mercy's sake.

Cases that tell people how to live their private lives arouse passionate controversy and are correspondingly difficult to settle, as the court found after its landmark 1973 *Roe v. Wade* decision legalizing abortion. There are 10,000 other patients like Cruzan

[1]Article by Nancy Gibbs, staff writer, from *Time* 135:62–71 Mr 19 '90. Copyright © 1990 by Time, Inc. Reprinted with permission.

in the U.S., and their families are waiting and watching. "I'm riding on the Cruzans' coattails," says St. Louis marketing consultant Pete Busalacchi, whose daughter Christine lies in the same Missouri rehabilitation center as Cruzan. "Maybe it would have been best if she had died that night," he says, referring to Christine's 1987 auto accident. "This has been a 34-month funeral." And like many Americans, Pete Busalacchi believes a family's private tragedy should not be a battleground for right-to-life interest groups, politicians or judges. "This is for individuals," he insists. "My suggestion is to take Nancy to the Supreme Court and wheel her in and ask, 'Do you want to live like this?'"

At the moment, most Americans seem to agree with Busalacchi. In a poll conducted last month for TIME/CNN by Yankelovich Clancy Shulman, 80% of those surveyed said decisions about ending the lives of terminally ill patients who cannot decide for themselves should be made by their families and doctors rather than lawmakers. If a patient is terminally ill and unconscious but has left instructions in a living will, 81% believe the doctor should be allowed to withdraw life-sustaining treatment; 57% believe it is all right for doctors in such cases to go even further and administer lethal injections or provide lethal pills.

Right-to-life advocates denounce what they call the "pro-death juggernaut," a shifting of public opinion on death and dying that is affecting not only private decisions but also public policy. Forty states and the District of Columbia have living-will laws that allow people to specify in advance what treatments they would find acceptable in their final days. In January, a New York State Supreme Court justice ruled that a family did not have to pay about two years' worth of $172-a-day fees for tending a comatose patient after they asked to have a feeding tube removed. That same month the Brooklyn district attorney decided not to press any charges against three grown children who had turned off their father's respirator, on the grounds that he was already brain dead.

Though statutes and court rulings may codify what is legal, they cannot ease the acute personal dilemmas of those who must deal directly with right-to-die situations. The issues that patients and families face are not only ethical but also medical, financial, legal and theological. In the last days of a ravaging disease, when the very technology that can save lives is merely prolonging death, how is a family to decide whether to stop the treatment? By adopting the abstract reasoning of jurists and ethicists weighing

legal arguments about privacy and moral arguments about mercy? Through some private intuition about how much sorrow they
can bear and how much courage they can summon? Or by some
blunt utilitarian calculation about whether it is more important to
keep Grandmother alive than to send Junior to college? In the
end, individuals are left with an intricate puzzle about what is
legal—and what is right—in making a decision.

It is not only families that must decide. Doctors are wonder-
ing when, in an era of untamed technology, they should stand
back and let their patients die—or even help death along. Econo-
mists are calculating a sort of social triage: at a time when infant
mortality is scandalously high and public health care is a sham-
bles, does it make sense for taxpayers to spend tens of thousands
of dollars a year to keep each unconscious patient alive? Lawmakers are struggling with how to draft laws carefully enough to
protect life while respecting individual choice. Theologians are
debating how sacred life can be if we take it upon ourselves to
end it.

It is not surprising that physicians are on the front lines of the
euthanasia debate, since they are the only participants for whom
life-and-death decisions are as common as they are complex.
They are most acutely conscious of the allocation of scarce
resources—time, money and their own energy—among patients
who might be cured and those who can only be sustained. And it
is they who must offer explanations to the anxious families of
patients whose lives are lost but not yet gone.

It is a basic premise of medicine that doctors should be heal-
ers and care givers; that they must work for their patients' well-
being; that if they cannot cure, they should at least do no harm.
When they took their Hippocratic oath, they promised, "I will
give no deadly medicine to anyone if asked, nor suggest any such
counsel . . ." But the plight of the incurably ill has challenged all
these premises and left doctors and nurses deeply divided over
their duties to the dying.

For many physicians, the actions they take often depend more
on circumstance than on moral certainty. How far is the patient
from death? How great is the pain? How clear the will? Does the
patient just want to be left alone, or is he asking to be killed? The
Cruzan case has raised the basic medical issue of whether doctors
must continue to treat patients they cannot cure. In its amicus
brief to the Supreme Court, the American Academy of Neurol-

ogy argues that the doctor's duty is to continue treating unconscious patients as long as there is some chance of improvement,
which Nancy Cruzan does not have. When hope is gone, the duty
ends. But the Association of American Physicians and Surgeons
argues precisely the opposite. "The obligation of the physician to
the comatose, vegetative, or developmentally disabled patient
does not depend upon the prospect for recovery," it wrote in its
brief. "The physician must always act on behalf of the patient's
well-being."

Taken to the extreme, this principle can mean ignoring or
overriding the patient's express wishes. When Dax Cowart was
critically burned in a propane-gas explosion near Henderson,
Texas, he begged a passing farmer for a gun with which to kill
himself. On his way to the hospital, he pleaded with the medic to
let him die. For weeks his life hung by a thread. For more than a
year, against his will, he endured excruciating treatment: his right
eye and several fingers were removed, his left eye was sewn shut.
His pain and his protests were unrelenting. One night he crawled
out of bed to try to throw himself out a window, but was discovered and prevented.

That was 17 years ago. Cowart is now a law school graduate,
married, living in Texas and managing his investments. Yet to this
day he argues that doctors violated his right to choose not to be
treated. "It doesn't take a genius to know that when you're in that
amount of pain, you can either bear it or you can't," he says. "And
I couldn't." He still resents the powerlessness of patients who are
forced to live when they beg to die. "The physicians say that when
a patient is in that much pain, he is not competent to make judgments about himself. It's the pain talking. And then when narcotics are given to subdue the pain, they say it's the narcotics talking.
It's a no-win situation."

In Cowart's case, doctors acted paternalistically; they over-
ruled his pleas in the belief that he would one day recover sufficiently to be grateful. But what if there were no chance of recovery: no law school, no wedding, no "life" down the road? Are
doctors still obliged to fight on for their patients, even in a losing
battle, even against their will? When a patient's time is short and
his wishes are clear, many doctors these days would say no to life-
at-all-costs heroics. Overtreatment of the terminally ill strikes
physicians as both wasteful and inhumane. And patients living
within sight of death often find themselves more concerned with
the quality of the life that remains than with its quantity. Once

reconciled to the inevitable, they want to die with dignity, not tethered to a battery of machines in an intensive-care unit like a laboratory specimen under glass.

When her cancer was diagnosed three years ago, Diana Nolan did not need much imagination or prophecy to know what lay ahead. The disease had killed both her parents. Surgeons removed part of her lung, but the cancer spread. Her physician next suggested that she try a potent chemotherapy but warned of the potential side effects—hair loss, nausea and vomiting. "I wanted a full week to think and pray," she recalls. "I am a person who wants to have a part in the treatment. Let me know what my options are." In the end, she told her doctor she wanted only pain-killers. Her two grown sons supported her decision, but some friends urged that she battle on. "They said, 'Go for it at all costs,' but I had seen my father, my mother and several friends go through this." She preferred to stay at home to die, and summoned her Episcopal priest to administer unction. Nolan hopes she will leave a message for those considering decisions like hers. "I wish people wouldn't be frightened about knowing what they're up against. To have a part in my treatment has been so important. I'm part of the team too."

But when doctors cannot consult the patient directly, the issue becomes much harder. Karen Ann Quinlan's was the most celebrated right-to-die case before Cruzan's, and one that seems almost straight-forward by comparison. In 1975, after she had been comatose for seven months, Quinlan's father went to the New Jersey Supreme Court to have her respirator turned off. The court agreed, and the U.S. Supreme Court declined to consider the case further. After the ruling, Quinlan lived nine more years breathing on her own. But Nancy Cruzan is not on a life-support system. Her parents are asking doctors to remove a feeding tube. If that petition is granted, Cruzan is sure to die within weeks, if not days.

When it is not high technology but rather basic care that is being withheld, doctors find themselves on shakier ground. Right-to-life proponents, including some physicians, argue that food and water, even supplied artificially, are not "medical treatment." They are the very least that human beings owe one another—and that doctors owe their patients. To keep a heart beating after a brain is dead makes no sense. But Nancy Cruzan is not brain dead; like a baby, she survives on her own if fed.

This distinction can put families and health-care workers at odds, as Robert Hayner found when he went to court in Albany to have his unconscious Aunt Elsie's medication stopped and the feeding tube removed. "How can we be expected to provide care if the tube is pulled?" demanded staff members at her nursing home in a court deposition. "How can we stand by and watch her starve to death? We are her family," they said. "We care about her. We cannot walk down the hall knowing we are killing her."

If doctors and nurses are uncomfortable about withholding food and water, they are profoundly uneasy about actively assisting a suicide. Yet a seemingly inexorable logic enters the picture: once it is acceptable to stand by and allow a patient to die slowly, why is it not more merciful to end life swiftly by lethal injection? What was once taboo is now openly discussed in academic journals: last March the *New England Journal of Medicine* published an article by twelve prominent physicians called "The Physician's Responsibility Toward Hopelessly Ill Patients." "It is difficult to answer such questions," the doctors wrote, "but all but two of us believe that it is not immoral for a physician to assist in the rational suicide of a terminally ill patient."

While such articles challenge doctors to rethink their professional roles, there is no agreement among them on this issue. Some physicians and ethicists warn that active euthanasia, if commonly practiced, could undermine the whole ethos of healing and the doctors' role as care givers. "A patient could never be totally confident that the doctor was coming to help him and not kill him," argues George Annas, director of the Law, Medicine & Ethics Program at Boston University's Schools of Medicine and Public Health.

Even hospice workers, who are more concerned with controlling pain than delaying death, are firmly opposed to the idea of loading a syringe with an overdose of morphine and handing it over. And doctors who spend all their time treating the incurably ill may still stop short of sanctioning euthanasia. "I don't want that word and my name in the same sentence," says Jeffrey Buckner, medical director for the Jacob Perlow Hospice of Beth Israel Medical Center in New York City. "If you are a physician and that charge is made against you, it sticks."

One of his patients, a 66-year-old writer suffering from a gastrointestinal cancer, came seeking help in committing suicide. He said he had the pills: 60 capsules, 200 mg each, of Seconal. But surgery left him with trouble swallowing, and he wondered if there was a better way to go. In this case it was not so much the physical pain of the cancer that plagued him; it was the mental burden of a lingering illness. "This long farewell performance gets to be a drag on people," the patient said. "It's just not the way you want to see yourself behaving. There's less dignity. Christ, everybody dies. Why does that always have to be the topic of conversation?" Dr. Buckner refused to help with a suicide. "It is reasonable to want to protect yourself from a horrible death," he explains. "But if good medical care is provided, and good pain relief, then those fears can be greatly alleviated."

For active help with a suicide, most patients will have to look elsewhere, well outside the realm of patient care. The spread of AIDS, for instance, has prompted some right-to-die activists to offer support and counseling about pills and occasionally lethal injections to people with the virus. Pierre Ludington, 44, executive director of the American Association of Physicians for Human Rights, has tested HIV-positive: he is stockpiling pills to use when he is ready to go. "I get angry that society wants me to suffer in a hospital," he says. "All I'm doing is feeding its coffers."

Ludington has his own idea of a death with dignity. "I envision having a wonderful meal with friends. After they leave, I'll sit in front of the fire listening to Mozart, mix everything with brandy, sip it, and somebody will find me." He is an eloquent if unlikely spokesman for the allocation debate. "I feel that money belongs to a symphony," he says, "or for an impoverished museum to buy a painting that lasts. I won't last. I won't last. It's an unconscionable act to keep me going."

Purely economic arguments for euthanasia can sound brutally calculating. But as health-care costs rise annually at double and triple the rate of inflation, and as new technologies promise ever higher bills for ever older patients, the questions grow about how to ration medical care. In 1987 the Oregon legislature voted to deny organ transplants under its Medicaid program and to use that money instead for prenatal care. It is only a matter of time before the issue of continuing care for patients in a vegetative state comes under similar scrutiny.

Jurists and ethicists wrestle with the wider implications of measuring the value of life on a sliding scale. Once a society agrees that at some stage a life is no longer worth sustaining, patients are suddenly vulnerable. "We would begin with competent people making their own choice," warns Daniel Callahan, director of the Hastings Center and an authority on ethical issues in medicine, "but we would be too easily led into involuntary euthanasia—either manipulating people into asking for suicide or actually doing it to them without their permission because they have become too burdensome or costly." The haunting precedent, of course, is the Nazi Holocaust, during which the chronically ill, then the socially unacceptable, and finally all non-Germans were viewed as expendable. In his stark essay "The Humane Holocaust," Christian author Malcolm Muggeridge notes that "it took no more than three decades to transform a war crime into an act of compassion."

As the historic taboo about mercy killing gradually erodes, the courts and legislatures are struggling to be sure that the vulnerable are protected—that, in the case of the severely disabled, the right to die not become a duty to die. They fear, for example, that medical care for newborn babies may come to depend on some cost-benefit analysis of their chance of living a "full healthy and active life." In the Baby Doe case in 1982, the Indiana courts allowed a couple to refuse surgery for their baby born with Down's syndrome and an incomplete esophagus; after six days, the baby starved to death. That emotional case raised the concern that some hospitals were not recommending even routine treatment for babies with Down's syndrome, spina bifida, cerebral palsy and other serious but treatable disabilities.

Both the medical and economic arguments for euthanasia are rejected by the powerful right-to-life movement, which commands hundreds of thousands of supporters nationwide. And as on the abortion issue, their stance against mercy killing is based on a theology that places the entire debate in a different context, that of a family of faith that tends most lovingly to its weakest members. The sanctity of a human existence, they argue, does not depend on its quality or its cost. What God gives only he can take away, and to usurp that right is an act of grave hubris. "Our Lord healed the sick, raised Lazarus from the dead, gave back sanity to the deranged," writes Muggeridge, "but never did He practice or envisage killing as part of the mercy that held possession of His heart."

But even within the community of faith there is a vast gray area. Though suffering and death underlie Judeo-Christian theology, basic compassion seems to dictate that a patient in terrible pain should be allowed to die. This is a proposition that the Roman Catholic Church appears to endorse. While both suicide and mercy killing are still strictly forbidden, the Vatican in 1980 declared that refusing treatment "is not equivalent to suicide; on the contrary, it should be considered as an acceptance of the human condition . . . or a desire not to impose excessive expenses on the family or community."

Even more active measures have their clerical champions. The late British Methodist clergyman Leslie Weatherhead rejected the idea that death should be left to God. "We do not leave birth to God," he observed. "We space births. We prevent births. We arrange births. Man should learn to become the lord of death as well as the master of birth." At the very least, argue some clerics, the state should stay out of the way. "The *Missouri* decision severs family ties," states a brief by the Evangelical Lutheran Church in America, referring to the ruling against the Cruzans, "by substituting the moral and religious judgment of the state for that of the person."

There is some irony here: the Evangelical Lutherans argue for a family's right to privacy, while the state of Missouri promotes the "sanctity of life." Yet the notion that life is sacred, and worthy of the state's protection, is embedded throughout the American legal tradition, right alongside the protection of individual liberty. When the two rights are at odds, the debates grow fierce. There are specific circumstances in which a society permits the intentional taking of life: in war, in self-defense, as punishment for a heinous crime. The Cruzan case raises the question of whether personal choice and great suffering, by either patients or their families, should join that set of circumstances.

Up until now the legal debate on the right to die has been wildly confused. If a car crashes on the George Washington Bridge and the driver is left comatose, his fate in court may depend on whether the ambulance takes him to New Jersey or New York. In New Jersey his family would probably be able to tell a hospital committee to stop life support. New York State's law is stricter, and without a living will the family would have to prove in court that the driver had left "clear and convincing evidence" that he would not want to be maintained by a machine.

But the laws are so unsettled that even in states where the statutes are strict, they may not necessarily be enforced. Judges and juries across the country have been remarkably lenient on family members who become mercy killers. Rudy Linares, a Chicago landscaper, held off hospital workers with a .357-cal. pistol while he unplugged his baby son's respirator. The 15-month-old boy died in his father's arms. Linares was charged with first-degree murder, but a Cook County grand jury refused to indict him. In fact, out of some 20 U.S. cases of "mercy killings" in the past 50 years, studied by Leonard Glantz of Boston University, only three defendants have been sentenced to jail.

The Cruzan case may finally provide the lower courts with some clear guidance in striking a fundamental balance between the rights of individuals and the duties of the state. If they chose, the Cruzans' lawyers could have suggested that Nancy's "life" is so faint that it does not meet a minimum standard of protection under the law; that, unaware as she is, she has none of those qualities and prospects and experiences that give life its value. But such an argument would require setting some line above which lives are protected, below which they are not. "In the public realm we need general rules that everyone in an institutional setting will follow," says Harvard political philosopher Robert Nozick. "And any line they draw will look arbitrary." Instead the case is being argued on the grounds of liberty and privacy.

The Cruzans' lawyers are asserting that Nancy's constitutional right to liberty has no meaning if it does not protect her from having a feeding tube surgically inserted in her stomach and being force-fed. Though she is unable to refuse the treatment, her parents could act on her behalf. Since the Karen Ann Quinlan case, 50 courts in 17 states have considered the right to have treatment withdrawn. Nearly all have come down on the side of privacy and limited the power of the government to dictate medical care. In a peculiar legal irony, many states make it illegal to assist in suicide; yet again and again, the courts have upheld the rights of conscious but paralyzed patients to have their ventilators and feeding tubes disconnected. In the most recent, highly publicized case, quadriplegic Larry James McAfee, still paralyzed five years after a motorcycle accident, petitioned the Georgia Supreme Court to allow him to disconnect his own ventilator using a special mouth-activated switch. Upholding McAfee's privacy rights, the court granted his petition. But McAfee subsequently decided not to end his life after all.

Unlike Georgia and many other states, however, Missouri has strong pro-life language in its statutes, which the state supreme court invoked in throwing out the lower-court decision. Though Cruzan had the right to refuse treatment, said the Missouri justices, her parents did not prove to the court that this is what she would have wanted. The "vague and unreliable" recollections by family and friends about Nancy's wishes were not deemed sufficient reason to stop feeding her. "The state's interest," wrote the judges, "is not in quality of life . . . Were quality of life at issue, all manner of handicaps might find the state seeking to terminate their lives. Instead, the state's interest is in life; that interest is unqualified."

Though no one questions the love of Cruzan's parents and their desire to abide by her wishes, what happens when a family's motives are not so clear? The state of Missouri is paying Cruzan's medical bills; but for other families the desire to hasten an inheritance or avoid crushing medical costs could add an ingredient of self-interest to a decision. The Rev. Harry Cole, a Presbyterian minister who faced the dilemma when his wife fell into a coma, admits the complexity of pressures. "If she were to go on that way, our family faced not only the incredible pain of watching her vegetate, but we also faced harsh practical realities." The cost of nursing-home care was likely to top $30,000 a year. "How could I continue to send three kids to college with the additional financial strain?"

The Cole case provides one more reason for courts to be careful about withdrawing life support: medicine is an uncertain science. When Cole's wife Jackie suffered a massive brain hemorrhage four years ago, the blood vessels in her brain ruptured, and she fell into a coma. "The vast majority of patients who have this kind of stroke die within a few hours," Dr. Tad Pula, the head of Maryland General Hospital's division of neurology, told Cole. But Jackie did not die right away; after several crises she stabilized into a vegetative state, which doctors said could last indefinitely. After talking with his children, Cole went to court to remove the respirator. But Baltimore Circuit Court Judge John Carroll Byrnes stayed his decision. Six days later, Jackie Cole woke up.

Today Jackie and Harry still appear on the talk-show circuit. She suffers some short-term memory loss, but otherwise is fully recovered. "When I look back at what the doctors said, I think, 'How wrong they were,'" she says. "What happened to me was truly miraculous." She does not blame Harry for wanting to pull the plug. "I know he loves me. I know he was never trying to do away with me." But the story does highlight the dilemma both judges and family members face. "I thought my decision was well planned, well thought out, responsible," says Cole. "It was what Jackie had asked me to do."

Such situations essentially confront families with a Hobson's choice: either they stand by and allow a loved one to waste away, or else they act to hasten death, with all the guilt and recrimination that entails. A state attorney accused 87-year-old Ruth Hoffmeister of wanting to starve her husband to death. Every evening for the past six years, Ruth has spoon-fed her husband Edward, who has Alzheimer's disease. When he began losing weight, their Pompano Beach, Fla., nursing home would have been obliged by state regulations to force-feed him through a tube. Ruth protested the bureaucratic intrusion. "There is nothing so important to an Alzheimer's patient," she insisted, "as a familiar touch and a familiar voice." She went to court to stop them, and won. "I don't know what the next step will be," she says. "After he had the disease for three years, he said to me, 'I am so tired of dying.' How could I ever justify keeping him alive?"

Although the wishes of patients and their families are often frustrated in court, lawmakers are not insensitive to their plight. Missouri Attorney General William Webster, who has led the legal fight against the Cruzans, may end up their unlikely ally. Webster realizes that few people have living wills, and that the Cruzans' ordeal has been torturous. "Without her case," he says, "I don't think people sitting in their living rooms would have to come face to face with the fact that we have thousands of patients across the country who are never going to recover. They are in this legal, medical nightmare—this limbo."

Webster endorses new legislation that would try to find a careful resolution. He has already met stiff resistance from the Missouri legislature and has a hard fight ahead to change the laws. He proposes that families of patients who have been continuously unconscious for three or more years could petition for withdrawing treatment, including food and water. If they were unanimous that this is what the patient would want, and three independent physicians certified that the coma was irreversible, the patient would be allowed to die.

That would put the decision back in the families' hands and leave them with the ultimate, intimate reckoning—a weighing of needs and fears and risks and possibilities. Long after the decision is made, the resolution may continue to haunt. But, in a sense, the abiding difficulty of these choices has a value of its own. It reflects the deep desire to do the right thing and respect the wishes of a loved one—and also an unshakable sense that life is neither to be taken nor relinquished lightly, even in mercy's name.

LAST RIGHTS[2]

Marie was dying. Her 69-year-old body, wasted by incurable emphysema and inoperable lung cancer, could no longer function on its own. As her family stood by her hospital bedside on a hot summer morning, the doctor suggested hooking her up to life-sustaining equipment. Marie looked beseechingly at her daughter Rose. "What do you think?" she asked. "No, Mom," Rose answered. Marie nodded. The doctor bristled. "If that were *my* mother, I'd do it," he said. But the family stood firm. The following day Marie died quietly, without the whirs, clicks and high-tech hums that form an electronic dirge for so many Americans. Last week Rose explained why she was buying *Final Exit*, Derek Humphry's controversial new best-selling guide to suicide. "I don't want what happened to me to happen to my children, to have a doctor try to dictate to them," she said. "It's an outrage. When I'm dying, *I* want to be in control."

Whose death is it anyway? More and more people—whether they are terminally ill, know someone who is, or are simply confronting their own mortality—are asking that question. To die in America is no longer simple. Before the 1950s, most patients died at home. Now they may spend their final days (or months or years) in a hospital or nursing home, often attached to sophisticated machinery that can extend even the most fragile life. "Doctors have always been in control, but now it's not just doctors and patients," Ruth Macklin, professor of bioethics at Albert Einstein College of Medicine in New York City, says. "There are hospital administrators, in-house attorneys and risk managers . . . These are the people who are *really* in control." To circumvent that tangled bureaucracy, to avoid the crushing burden of extended illness, many people now consider the possibility of taking life— and death—into their own hands.

Bookstores can't keep *Final Exit* in stock; almost 150,000 cop-

[2]Article by Katrine Ames, staff writer, from *Newsweek* 118:40–41 Ag 26 '91. Copyright © 1991 by Newsweek, Inc. Reprinted with permission.

ies of the slim, $16.95 volume are on order. Before "right to die" entered the lexicon, before Karen Anne Quinlan, Nancy Cruzan and Dr. Jack Kevorkian became familiar names, *Final Exit* would have been unimaginable. Only 41 percent of the respondents in a 1975 Gallup poll said they believed that someone in great pain, with "no hope of improvement," had the moral right to commit suicide. By 1990, that figure had risen to 66 percent. Derek Humphry, president of The Hemlock Society, a euthanasia organization founded in 1980, thought the time was right for a "responsible" suicide manual. Though *Final Exit* is straightforward, it is not an emotionless directive. "I wanted it to say, 'Be considerate of others, go careful with your life and other people's feelings'," Humphry says. A man whose ailing, elderly parents committed suicide after reading *Final Exit* wrote to Humphry: "For what it is worth, we thank you for providing accurate information and advice."

Though *Final Exit* proposes an extreme measure for ending life, it speaks to a growing concern of most Americans. With continuing advances in medical technology, the prospect of being kept alive—perhaps insentient—by machinery is real and frightening. About 1.3 million Americans die annually in hospitals, hundreds of thousands more in nursing homes; many end their lives with a negotiated death. More and more people are asking what they can and should do *now* to try to ensure a dignified, humane death. There are several documents which can help, but the laws governing them are patchwork. Speak to a lawyer, a doctor and your family.

• **Living Will:** outlines what medical treatment you want—or do not want—should you no longer be able to express your wishes. Its legal limits vary; fill in one for the state in which you live.

• **Health-Care Proxy:** designates an agent—a friend or family member—to act for you in health-care matters. It is often included within a living will and, like it, may have limited powers. For example, it may cover only terminal illness, which would not include a coma or Alzheimer's disease.

• **Durable Power of Attorney for Health Care:** a more inclusive document that permits your agent to act for you in most health-care matters, including those you might not have considered.

Most Americans—84 percent, according to a 1990 Gallup poll—say that if they were on life-support systems and had no hope of recovering, they would want treatment withheld. Like diabetics or heart patients, they can purchase Medic Alert bracelets, but theirs are emblazoned LIVING WILL/DO NOT RESUSCITATE. "There has been an extraordinary decline in trust between physicians and patients, and patients and hospitals," says David Rothman, author of "Strangers at the Bedside" and professor of social medicine at Manhattan's Columbia College of Physicians and Surgeons. "People don't believe that the hospital will do what they want."

Under the full glare of the media, courts and medical journals are debating right-to-die decisions. Says Dr. Robert McAfee, a Portland, Maine, surgeon and vice chairman of the American Medical Association's board of trustees, "Our social contract is to sustain life and relieve suffering. But sometimes these ideals are in conflict." They were for Dr. Timothy Quill, an internist in Rochester, N.Y. Last March, in The New England Journal of Medicine, he wrote movingly of how he helped a leukemia patient stockpile barbiturates so she could take her own life: "I [had] an uneasy feeling about the boundaries I was exploring—spiritual, legal, professional and personal. Yet I also felt strongly that I was setting her free to get the most out of the time she had left, and to maintain dignity and control on her own terms." Last month a Rochester grand jury refused to indict Quill on criminal charges, including manslaughter. Still, some worry that patients may not make informed choices about when and how to die. "I feel a great deal of discomfort about how comfortable people have become with [euthanasia]," says Carol Gill, director of psychological research at the Chicago Institute of Disability Research. "I take a very suspicious view of 'voluntariness' in these issues."

We may never be able to codify the complex ethics of medical technology. There are, however, changes afoot. A new federal law, the Patient Self-Determination Act of 1990, goes into effect this December: it will require hospitals participating in Medicare or Medicaid to ask all adult inpatients if they have "advance directives" such as living wills. In Washington state, legalized euthanasia is a possibility. The November ballot will carry an initiative with an "aid in dying" provision that would allow doctors to help the mentally competent, terminally ill die. Patients could request help in writing at the time they want to die. Two witnesses would have to certify that the request is voluntary.

Most of us have some choice in how we live, certainly in how we conduct our lives. How we die is an equally personal choice— and, in the exhilarating and terrifying new world of medical technology—perhaps almost as important.

DEAD COMPLICATED[3]

In a recent test case, a Florida couple sued a local hospital to have their doomed newborn child declared dead. Their daughter Theresa was an anencephalic infant, born with only a brain stem, a tiny stump of a brain. Since virtually all her brain was missing, she would never be aware of her existence. In addition, her faltering heart and lungs were bound to give out in a matter of days. If she was pronounced dead, her parents would at least be able to donate her organs to help other sick infants survive. It was a reasonable request made by well-meaning parents. But a Florida circuit court rejected it on the grounds that the baby still had a brain stem. According to state law, she was therefore alive. Ten days later, while a fierce debate raged among doctors, ethicists, and lawyers, the infant's breathing stopped and her organs petered out for lack of oxygen, making them useless for transplantation.

As the sad case of baby Theresa demonstrates, the line between life and death is today often blurred. Once it was simple. A person was alive if his heart could beat and his lungs could breathe, and dead if they did not. It was an intuitive and satisfying definition. Who among us does not accept the *lub-dub* of a heart and the gentle rise and fall of a chest as reassuring signs of life? But now that machines can do the job of a heart or lung, these vital signs are no longer sufficient to define a living human being. Modern medicine has made the notion of heart-lung death increasingly inadequate, and we doctors must now rely on the much more abstract concept of brain death.

The idea was not immediately popular. Long after the first states adopted it in the early 1970s, others hung on to the traditional notion of heart-lung death, with absurd results. Ten years ago an intensive care patient being transferred from a hospital in Boston to one in Washington could have been alive in Massachusetts, dead in Connecticut, alive in New York and New Jersey, and dead again in D.C. These days, at least, there's greater consistency. Most states, including Florida, use a "whole brain" concept of death: that is, the person is dead if the entire brain, including the brain stem, has ceased to function.

[3]Article by Elisabeth Rosenthal, physician and columnist, from *Discover* 13:28–30 O '92. Copyright © 1992 by The Walt Disney Co. Reprinted with permission.

As in the case of baby Theresa, that has helped solve the legal dilemma of when to declare a patient dead, but it clearly hasn't resolved the question of when life ends in a way that satisfies the soul. Whole-brain death is diagnosed by an elaborate battery of neurological tests rather than by a gut instinct of what it means to be alive. And even doctors and nurses working in the twilight world of the intensive care unit may find it deeply disturbing that patients who are legally dead look from the outside just like patients who are legally alive.

A 1989 survey of doctors and nurses in Cleveland dramatically demonstrated the point. Most could define death as whole-brain death, all right. But in a written test many did not correctly identify whether the patients described were dead or alive. A quarter of the group identified a patient whose brain had ceased to function but whose heart was still pumping on life-support systems (legally dead) as alive! About an equal number declared dead a patient who was irreversibly unconscious but whose brain stem could still orchestrate basic functions like breathing (legally alive). That people who routinely witness death have trouble applying the definition of brain death to patients shows how poorly that definition fits with our intuitions and beliefs.

Indeed, in New York and New Jersey, lawmakers, under pressure from religious groups, have been forced to write an exemption to their statutes. A brain-dead practicing Catholic or Orthodox Jew can be treated as though alive, since his religious teachings hold that a beating heart is the benchmark of life.

The source of this subconscious resistance to brain death, I think, is clear. From an emotional standpoint it goes against the grain. And from a scientific standpoint, it's hard to define death at all when there's no well-defined minimum standard for membership in the club of human life. Is it having 23 chromosome pairs? A heartbeat? The ability to feel or think? Just as those involved in the abortion debate struggle to decide when life begins, doctors, ethicists, and legislators are struggling to decide when it ends. And as in the abortion debate, where they draw the line is often influenced by emotion, religious and moral beliefs, and politics.

Twenty-five years ago there was no such dilemma. Patients whose heart and lungs stopped quickly turned blue and pulseless and were declared dead. If their brain was destroyed by massive head injury, bleeding, or stroke, the heart and lungs succumbed as well since the lower part of the brain helps orchestrate their function. And then along came intensive care units, cardio-pulmonary resuscitation, respirators, and heart-bypass pumps. I recall one 60-year-old patient who had emphysema and severe heart rhythm problems; she needed a respirator to breathe and had an electric-shock machine implanted in her heart to reset the rhythm when the organ stopped pumping. Although her lungs were shot and her heart stopped many times, she read, knitted, and entertained guests in her hospital room. Clearly alive.

With machines to breathe and pump blood, a breathing chest and beating heart could no longer be the hallmark of life. And so doctors turned toward a brain-oriented definition of death. The advent of organ transplantation also exerted a powerful influence, since hearts, livers, and lungs for transplant must be removed from bodies with blood and oxygen still coursing through their veins. Nevertheless, defining brain death continues to engender controversy.

Scientific conservatives argue that the entire brain must die for a person to be dead, and this whole-brain concept was enacted into law. But this definition allows babies like Theresa and patients in deep, irreversible comas with just a scrap of brain function to be counted as alive. To some people this makes no sense. Anencephalics and patients in a so-called persistent vegetative state have only a brain stem, a stalk of brain that allows their bodies to perform basic, reflexive functions like breathing. But they will never be conscious, never see, feel, or think in even the most rudimentary fashion. Such functions are controlled by the cortex, the furrowed outer layer of the higher brain. Consequently some doctors argue that the death of the cortex reduces a being to a state that's less than human—a state of death. Therefore people in persistent vegetative states and anencephalic infants should be counted as dead and their organs released for donation.

Another problem with whole-brain death is that it's tricky to ascertain. Often it takes the specialized knowledge of a neurologist to distinguish the person in an irreversible coma who is alive from the person in an irreversible coma who is dead—the key distinction being a functioning brain stem.

Many of the brain stem's duties involve extremely primitive reflexes: insuring that we breathe, move our eyes in a coordinated manner, blink when something grazes our eye. These simple maneuvers require great ingenuity to test in the intensive care unit. Patients who are unconscious and therefore unseeing do not look around to demonstrate eye coordination. And how do you tell if a patient's chest is moving air in a place where everyone is hooked up to breathing machines?

To test eye movements, neurologists resort to some bizarre tactics. For example, even in people who are deeply comatose, a good squirt of cold water in the ear causes the eyes to twitch uncontrollably toward the invaded ear. It is an extremely noxious stimulus (conscious patients will sense the world spinning and throw up), but it is a sure way to check that the brain stem is working.

To test breathing skill, doctors have devised an equally devious challenge called an apnea test. It is virtually impossible to tell if a person in a deep coma on a respirator can breathe just by turning off the machine. The centers in the brain stem that direct the lungs to take a breath sense high levels of carbon dioxide, a waste product of the body's metabolism, rather than low levels of oxygen, the essential gas that we all need.

When a comatose patient's respirator is turned off, the oxygen level begins to fall and the CO_2 level climbs. Since CO_2 is not terribly toxic to organs, the brain is programmed to allow high levels to build up before it panics and directs the body to take a breath. And, unfortunately, the oxygen content of blood often dips to deadly levels before the CO_2 rises high enough to sound the brain-stem alarm. So—catch-22—if a doctor seeks to diagnose death by turning off a respirator, his search will become a self-fulfilling prophecy.

To avoid killing the patient in an attempt to determine if he is dead, doctors give comatose patients 100 percent oxygen to breathe through a ventilator for 10 to 20 minutes and then place a tube blowing a constant flow of oxygen into the airway leading to the lungs. They saturate the patient with oxygen, so that even if the body does not seek to breathe after the ventilator is turned off, the vital organs can survive. Under these conditions, the body is given 10 minutes to take a breath in response to the rising CO_2 after the ventilator is turned off. If it does, the patient is alive; if not, he is dead. It is a pretty elaborate subterfuge to figure out what should be obvious.

The point struck home during my training when I cared for a 50-year-old woman who had been sent into a persistent vegetative state by a ruptured aneurysm in her brain. She developed lung problems while on a ventilator and, after she came off the machine, remained prone to pneumonia. Each time a new infection imperiled oxygen flow to her brain, she came back to intensive care to be put on a respirator. And each time we called in a neurologist to determine if lack of oxygen had killed off the brain stem to render her dead. Although my patient looked exactly the same, the first three times the answer was no, but the fourth time it was yes.

Apart from the absurdity of situations like these, the insistence that every last brain cell must expire before a patient can be declared dead has also limited the supply of donor organs. A fragment of a brain stem can allow a patient to take some breaths, but (as was the case with baby Theresa) the breathing is often not sufficient to sustain vital organs.

That's another reason why a vocal minority of doctors have suggested that a patient needs some brain function above the primitive brain stem to qualify as a living human being—and that anything less makes him dead. Logic tells me they're right: if a beating heart does not suffice for us to be human beings, what is left but consciousness to link us all together?

Ethicists, of course, worry about a world in which a society chooses which parts of the brain are necessary to qualify an individual as human. If today we decide that a person in a persistent vegetative state is obviously not one of us, then tomorrow why not the woman who is severely retarded, or the man rendered speechless and immobile by a stroke? Having treated patients in all three states, it seems to me that there are clear distinctions. Even people who are severely retarded or paralyzed can experience something—can sense touch or taste food or feel pleasure. But in the endless coma of anencephaly or a persistent vegetative state, there is nothing.

So, were I to lapse into a persistent vegetative state or have a child born without a higher brain, I would desperately want the organs taken for donation in the hope that they might help others live. But, having said that, would I want society to allow me, as a practicing physician, to act on these instincts by declaring all patients with these conditions dead? Now I balk.

Although science and logic say these patients are dead, emotion shouts, no, they're alive! When I touch them, they're warm. When I place a stethoscope on their rising chests, I hear air moving and the vibrant beating of their hearts. George Annas, a lawyer at the Boston University School of Public Health, argues for a commonsense solution. "Dead is when you'd bury someone," he says. "To me the way to resolve the issue is to decide whether you'd bury someone with a beating heart. And the answer is no. In our society, being buried alive is the ultimate fear."

I have to agree. I just can't see putting people whose hearts are still beating and whose lungs are still breathing six feet under in a box—no matter how hopelessly comatose they may be. And with only a brain stem, those feats can in some fashion be performed.

So, reluctantly, I conclude that baby Theresa was alive and had to be allowed to die. Too bad we lost her organs.

III. DR. KEVORKIAN AND ASSISTED SUICIDE

EDITOR'S INTRODUCTION

The Hemlock Society was founded by Derek Humphry, a British journalist, in Los Angeles in 1980. The organization advocated active euthanasia, or aiding the death of a hopelessly ill individual. Anne Fadiman, in the first article, from *Harper's*, describes Humphry, the group, and the *Hemlock Quarterly*, its newsletter, which by 1988 was listing the lethal dose of eighteen commonly prescribed drugs. In 1991, Humphry published *Final Exit*, a manual on suicide, which quickly became a best-seller.

Also in the early 1990s, Dr. Jack Kevorkian became a national figure by continually defying legal statutes and assisting chronically ill patients to die. Nancy Gibbs's *Time* article reports on the public support for Kevorkian, and the medical profession's inadequacy in treating the pain of the dying.

Initiatives to legalize physician-assisted suicide in California, Washington, and Oregon is the topic of the next article, from *Commonweal*, by Courtney S. Campbell. The Oregon initiative only allows a physician to prescribe a lethal dose of drugs, leaving the act of suicide up to the patient. Moreover, the initiative would apply only to residents of the state suffering from an incurable illness that, with reasonable certainty, would result in death within six months. William McCord, writing in *The Humanist*, reveals that although favored in polls, the initiatives in California and Washington were defeated when elections were held. (The Oregon initiative, however, was approved by voters in November 1994.) Many voters cited the sanctity of life as the reason for their opposition, but McCord concludes that euthanasia, such as it is practiced in the Netherlands, does not debase human life, but rather serves the cause of human dignity and autonomy.

DEATH NEWS[1]

The *Hemlock Quarterly,* an unassuming little newsletter that until recently was the chief perquisite of membership in the Hemlock Society, may have been the only radical publication in the United States whose subscriber rolls were dominated by affluent white women with gray hair. I've met many of these women, and I can attest that they were the sort of community-minded grandmothers who never littered, never stole anyone's parking place, and always returned their library books on time. With the help of *HQ,* these model citizens laid down a store of knowledge that would enable them, if they so chose, to commit one or several felonies, from smuggling drugs over the U.S. border to aiding and abetting a suicide. Most of them, of course, subscribed to the newsletter in order to prepare for the perfectly legal expedient of killing themselves.

I recently learned that the last issue of 1993 would be *HQ*'s final edition. The *Hemlock Quarterly* was to be replaced by a bimonthly called *Time-Lines,* which would cover fast-breaking legislative news; a graphic artist was enlisted to effect a modest redesign; a public relations expert was consulted to attract a more influential audience of physicians, politicians, and academics—in short, the humble gadfly was going corporate. When I heard this, I decided to reread all fifty-three issues, the complete *HQ* oeuvre from 1980 to 1993. Perusing them one by one, every three months, had been like looking at a collection of still pictures. Reading them in rapid succession, in a two-day thanatological orgy, was like thumbing through a macabre flip-book that charted the entire course of the modern American right-to-die movement. As the *Hemlock Quarterly*'s swiftly evolving notions of what was morally acceptable flashed past, the face of Karen Ann Quinlan dissolved into that of Elizabeth Bouvia, who became, in turn, William Bartling, then Arthur and Cynthia Koestler, then Roswell Gilbert, and finally, like a grinning death's head, the face of Jack Kevorkian.

---

[1]Article by Anne Fadiman, recipient of a National Magazine Award in 1987 for her reportage on the right-to-die movement. From *Harper's* 288:74–80+ Ap '94. Copyright © 1994 by *Harper's Magazine.* Reprinted with permission.

The Hemlock Society's First Voluntary Euthanasia Conference was held in the spring of 1983 in a drafty Unitarian church on the outskirts of downtown San Francisco. In that innocent, pre-Kevorkian era, the Hemlock members were already old, tired, and none too healthy-looking, but the right-to-die movement was still young and pure. I was one of only two journalists present. The sound of rain against the stained-glass windows contributed to the atmosphere of reverent sobriety. The small audience of mostly female partisans huddled together in the front pews, umbrellas furled at their feet. This was a congregation far too decorous to shout "Hallelujah!" but a WASP susurration of assent swept through the nave of the church whenever one of the speakers formulated a particularly high-minded aphorism: "Let us value the quality of life, not the quantity." "Suicide ends the living process; euthanasia ends the dying process." The featured speaker was a professor of ethics who declared that although self-determination for the terminally ill was a praiseworthy cause—indeed, a sacred trust—the members of Hemlock must never compromise their moral probity by going too far. She referred to this concept as the Camel's Nose Argument. Once the camel's nose was under the tent, one had to take careful precautions to prevent the rest of the beast from following suit.

I remember thinking, as I looked around the church, that the camel didn't have a chance. I had expected a cell of wide-eyed sansculottes and had found, instead, a genteel sorority of senior citizens. I was sure they would never let their movement go anywhere untoward. In fact, I wondered if they had the chutzpah to let it go much of anywhere at all.

That night, however, I lay on my motel bed and idly scanned a copy of the *Hemlock Quarterly* that I had picked up on my way out of the church. It was printed on cheap, uncoated, canary-yellow paper—an "up" color, as Hemlock's founder, Derek Humphry, explained to me later, "because although we support self-deliverance, we don't want to seem a death-and-doom type of an organization." Its logo was the Rx symbol superimposed over a hemlock plant. Though the *Hemlock Quarterly* looked like something that might be published by a particularly unsophisticated PTA, I knew before I had reached the second page that I had found the true cradle of the revolution.

Most of the presentations at the Hemlock conference had been about passive euthanasia, or letting people die: hospices, living wills, plug-pulling. The *Hemlock Quarterly* was miles ahead.

It advocated active euthanasia, or *helping* people die. Its lead article was headlined LET DOCTORS SUPPLY LETHAL DRUGS. Lest this seem too avant-garde a concept, the newsletter slyly reprinted a concurring opinion on the subject, dated 1516. (In Sir Thomas More's *Utopia,* the victim of a painful, incurable disease, convinced he was already leading "a sort of posthumous existence," could be "given a soporific and put painlessly out of his misery.") The conference had dealt in abstract principles; *HQ* dealt in the real miseries that real people wanted to be put out of—quadriplegia, dementia, lung cancer, breast cancer, brain cancer, stomach cancer, ovarian cancer, Parkinson's disease, amyotrophic lateral sclerosis, macular degeneration, emphysema, strokes, colostomies, catheters, bedpans, bedsores. All of the conference speakers had hewed to the official Hemlock line, which sanctioned suicide only in cases of terminal illness; *HQ* intimated that terminal ignominy might sometimes be sufficient cause. The issue I had picked up featured two accounts by readers of the suicides of their elderly mothers. One woman, after trying unsuccessfully to kill herself by pressing on her jugular vein, spent thirty-three days starving herself to death; the other died from an overdose of painkillers. Though the self-starver was comforted in her final days by the scent of carnation leis and the sound of Beethoven's *Moonlight Sonata,* it was not hard to guess which death the editors favored. I had underestimated the members of Hemlock. In the pages of their newsletter, the camel was already in up to the first hump.

I've read *HQ* ever since, courtesy of Hemlock's unflagging media comp list. It arrived like clockwork every three months, a totally subversive little rag that seemed endearingly unaware of its own bizarreness. Though some of its subject matter was highly technical, the space it allotted to letters from readers lent it a *cozy* tone, a kind of kaffeeklatsch approach to self-annihilation. In its homely pages, moral questions that had traditionally been co-opted by philosophers were returned to the more experienced hands of M.B., of Laguna Hills, California, and Mrs. F., of Arizona. The pleasures *HQ* afforded me were entirely voyeuristic—I was young and healthy and knew nothing of suffering—but I liked and trusted M.B. and Mrs. F., and I always looked forward to the newsletter's arrival, even though it always made me sad.

The Hemlock Society was launched in Los Angeles in the summer of 1980 by Derek Humphry, a British journalist who had helped his terminally ill first wife take her own life, and Ann Wickett, Humphry's second wife, an American academic. The name was Wickett's idea. She and Humphry agreed it had a noble Socratic ring, although they did not recommend hemlock as a suicide method, since it can cause painful convulsions. The society's general counsel advised Humphry to spread his gospel of peaceful self-deliverance via the printed word; the First Amendment would be Hemlock's shield. Thus was the *Hemlock Quarterly* born. Its maiden issue appeared in October 1980. Humphry and Wickett edited it, wrote most of it, laid it out in their garage, trundled it around the corner to a printer of wedding and bar mitzvah invitations, and licked all the stamps themselves. It had 443 subscribers, most of whom had contacted Humphry after Hemlock's first press conference. Its final issue had 39,463. *HQ* never put on airs: though it grew from five pages to fourteen, though its paper stock changed from yellow to white, though its typeface enlarged to accommodate the uncertain eyesight of its elderly readers, the fifty-third issue of the quarterly looked just as rinky-dink as the first.

During the thirteen years that elapsed between issue No. 1 and issue No. 53, the right-to-die movement passed a succession of extraordinary milestones that *HQ* both recorded and influenced. If any matter concerning euthanasia appeared on the front page of the *New York Times,* one could be certain that it had already been reported—sometimes years earlier—by the *Hemlock Quarterly.* The very first issue contained a bellwether article about physician aid-in-dying in the Netherlands. Six months before Dr. Kevorkian facilitated his first suicide, *HQ* ran a brief profile of him and noted that he would be the next speaker featured by Hemlock's Michigan chapter. When Robert Harper, the first Hemlock member to be charged with murder, was tried for assisting his wife's suicide, *HQ* not only covered the case but raised $14,000 to pay the defense team Hemlock had engaged. Harper, who wore a Hemlock GOOD LIFE, GOOD DEATH pin throughout his trial, was acquitted.

In addition to covering news, *HQ* reviewed books, movies, and plays with suicidal themes; published jokes about terminal illness; ran obituaries of prominent suicides, noting with pride if the deceased had used a Hemlock-approved method of self-deliverance; printed the addresses of inmates convicted of mercy killings so that Hemlock members could send them sympathy cards; and, aware that it was blessed with an elderly readership with bequests on their minds, solicited contributions ("All gifts, donations, legacies to the Hemlock Society are tax deductible under 501c3 of the IRS tax code"). *HQ* also offered Hemlock videos for $20 ("ideal to show friends"); GOOD LIFE, GOOD DEATH posters for $6 ("a striking wall decoration"); and publications ("Why not give some of Hemlock's books as Christmas presents this year?").

The *Hemlock Quarterly* did not merely report to its readers; it actively courted their participation. The very first issue noted that "each of us has a story to tell; by sharing it we can all grow." The letters department functioned as a community bulletin board that allowed Hemlock members, even those who would never again leave their beds, to get acquainted, lend one another support, trade advice, and complain about their infirmities (but never to excess, because they were chin-up sorts). Mary K., of New Jersey, the victim of a paralytic stroke, noted briskly that the essentials of her life were "Shakespeare, a bedpan, soap, water, and wash cloths, in that order." J.B., of Pennsylvania, who was afflicted with degenerative muscular atrophy and fecal incontinence, noted, "I freeze vegetables all summer from my husband's garden; I go out for dinner or Atlantic City Casinos when my bowels allow me." Both women ended their testimonies by saying that if they became further incapacitated, they wanted the option of suicide. Even those *HQ* readers whose health was not yet precarious let it be known that they were keeping a weather eye on their futures. Gloria Moorer, of Tacoma, Washington, whose mother had died a lingering death, wrote that she had failed to obtain liquid morphine for her own stockpile and had therefore turned to high-risk sports:

When I began to be concerned about the possibility of suffering a similar fate to my mother's, I decided to take up every dangerous physical activity that I could think of. I learned to down hill ski at 50, to windsurf at 55, to roller skate at 60, and I started cross country biking this spring at 64. . . . I kept thinking I'll go over a cliff, or drown at sea having a wonderful adventure, and instead, I get healthier and healthier! There is a terrible irony here, as my fear is not of dying, but of dying slowly. Can you suggest any solution for me if my doctor doesn't buy the insomnia routine?

Some readers simply wished to share cheerful stories about family members who had made their exits after drinking champagne, eating blueberry yogurt, listening to favorite pieces of classical music, or, in the case of the mother of J.R., of Canada, reciting the Twenty-third Psalm before she took a dose of barbiturates and was asphyxiated by a plastic bag her daughter had secured with a silk scarf. "On occasion," noted J.R., "I still wear that same silk scarf, with pride."

To fathom why nearly 40,000 readers spent $25 a year for four measly issues, you need to understand the genre of periodical to which *HQ* belonged. You might be tempted to compare it with other journals that have political agendas, such as, say, *International Socialism* or *Libertarian Digest,* but that would be a misconstruction of its true nature. *HQ* was really a how-to magazine, like *Needlepoint News* or *Bon Appétit.* Its readers were recipe clippers. They were seeking a recipe they would use only once, but whose ingredients, and methods of preparation and consumption, had to be nothing less than perfect.

The editors of *HQ* knew this from the start, but in the newsletter's early days, they were prohibitively fearful of being prosecuted for furnishing the instructions their readers craved. The first year of *HQ*'s publication, 1980, was a dangerous time for suicide promoters. Hemlock's British analogue, the EXIT Society, was in deep trouble: its general secretary had been charged with aiding and abetting suicide, and its executive committee was too scared to publish its *Guide to Self-Deliverance. HQ*'s early issues were full of nervous statements by Hemlock's attorney about "the risk of serious criminal charges" that the organization might run by merely advocating suicide as a responsible option for terminally ill patients, even if it didn't publish "any recipes or other procedural advice."

HQ ran no risks, of course, by telling its readers how *not* to commit suicide, so its editors filled many pages with methodological caveats. Because "most Hemlock members are gentle, civilized people and would not wish their loved ones to witness their bodies mutilated by gunfire," firearms were out. Hara-kiri was also advised against. Since I doubted that many Hemlock members had contemplated death by disembowelment and decapitation, I initially wondered why the editors deemed the subject worthy of coverage, especially in a full-page article so richly detailed as to seem almost prurient:

> In a very few cases hara-kiri was carried out without the ritual execution. In these cases the hara-kiri man cut the abdominal wall first and then cut the cervical artery next. This is very important because one cannot die of bleeding by cutting the abdominal wall only.

It occurred to me that the readers of *HQ* were not just potentially suicidal; they were *connoisseurs* of suicide. They might enjoy reading how to slice up an abdomen in the same armchair spirit as a subscriber to *Gourmet* might relish learning how to slice up a wild boar, knowing that it was so hard to buy, so hard to cook, and so laden with cholesterol that she would never actually make it.

Inch by inch, year by year, the camel crept into the tent. In the very beginning, *HQ* printed only vague references to "barbiturates" and "sedatives." Then, in 1981, it ran a short list of books in the public domain—*Toxicology, the Basic Science of Poisons; The Pharmacological Basis of Therapeutics;* and three others—that contained "information on bloodless and painless lethal methods of self-deliverance." The information, however, was available only to those readers willing and able to go to the library, read hundreds of pages of small print, and ferret out the relevant material. As time passed and no police came knocking at their door, *HQ*'s editors became incrementally more daring. Even if they could not publish recipes that looked like recipes, they realized that they could sneak the material into their newsletter by dressing it up in various respectable disguises. (Their determination to print drug dosages reminded me of Wolcott Gibbs's account of *Life* magazine's "bothersome and heroic struggle . . . to figure out a way to print a picture of a living, breathing woman with absolutely no clothes on" in their G-rated pages, a challenge to which they rose by photographing a life-drawing class at the Yale Art School.)

One of *HQ*'s favorite vehicles for suicide tips was its book reviews, which over the years must constitute one of the strangest bodies of literary criticism ever published. In a review of *Exit House,* a memoir by the artist Jo Roman, Derek Humphry casually mentioned "the final night when [Roman] took 4.5 grams of Seconal." Betty Rollin's *Last Wish* was praised for its writing but castigated for its pharmaceutical errors: ". . . the capsules specified in the book under the trade name Nembutal and of 100 milligram strength are described as 'shiny, red, gelatin-covered capsules, no bigger, each one, than the head of a match.' The 100 mg Nembutal capsules are a gold color (the only Nembutal which are even partially red are the 50 mg variety) and are much larger than any matchhead."

The most reliable Trojan horse for the conveyance of suicide formulas was the letters department. Eyewitness accounts of suicides, reprinted without comment, kept the editors' hands clean, the correspondents safely anonymous, and the readers apprised of how their fellow Hemlock members had handled situations they might in the not-too-distant future face themselves. A typical sample:

At the age of 89 years and five months, on a beautiful sunny afternoon, in a pretty feminine bedroom overlooking a patio of flowers that she had raised and tended for almost 20 years, my mother went peacefully to sleep as I sat and held her hand and talked her over the rainbow with relaxing Yoga meditations.

She gave me the gift of life and I gave her the gift of peace. Thanks also to you. Enclosed is a donation to your work.

My mother's prescription for death was one Dramamine (as antiemetic), then a 20 minutes wait, then tea and dry toast. Another 20 minute wait, then 25 Seconal of 100 mg rapidly taken and washed down with whiskey and soda.

Grateful member
(Name and address withheld)

In 1988, *HQ* finally threw caution to the winds and published a straightforward Drug Dosage Table listing the lethal dosages of eighteen common prescription drugs: Amytal, Butisol, Valium, Dalmane, Doriden, Noctec, Dilaudid, Miltown, Noludar, Demerol, Dolophine, Norflex, Seconal, Nembutal, Darvon, codeine, morphine, and phenobarbital. It was captioned: "*Only* for the information of members of the National Hemlock Society for possible self-deliverance from a future terminal illness. . . . *Keep this document in a secure, private place.*"

Knowing what dosages to take was of no help, of course, if *HQ*'s readers couldn't get the pills. One recommended avenue was faking insomnia to procure barbiturate prescriptions. Another option was traveling to foreign countries where some of the recommended drugs might be available without prescription. Like any tourists eager to share shopping tips, *HQ*'s readers sent in bulletins about their success in obtaining phenobarbital in Bangkok or Norflex in Vancouver. Mexico was the favored—though not a foolproof—drug mecca. Henry L. Brod, of Florida, wrote that he and his wife, equipped with "the immensely useful January 1988 *Hemlock Quarterly*," in which the Drug Dosage Table had been printed, "flew to Merida, in the Yucatan, and decided to mix holiday with some research into the availability of drugs rumored to be easily available 'over the counter.'" Alas, although the Brods did find some phenobarbital, their tour of seventeen *farmacias* yielded no Seconal, Nembutal, or Demerol, and their vacation was cut short when Mrs. Brod contracted a severe case of Montezuma's revenge.

Even if the readers of *HQ* did manage to obtain the right drugs, even if they stored them properly in 35-millimeter film cans ("Make sure the little cap is fastened tightly"), and even if they enhanced their toxicity with alcohol, death still was not guaranteed. They might lose consciousness before they swallowed the full dose. They might vomit. If they had built up a tolerance to medications they had been taking regularly, they might need more pills than they had anticipated. The only fail-safe technique was to back up the drugs with a belt-and-braces policy; namely, a plastic bag. The very idea seems to make many people—even Hemlock members—queasy, partly because suffocation is such a universal fear, partly because a person with a bag on his head doesn't look like himself, and partly because plastic bags are so cheap, so banal, so housewifely, as if Tupperware had been discovered to have lethal properties.

During *HQ*'s first eight years, the editors considered the notion of plastic bags so unsavory as to be virtually unmentionable. Then, in 1988, in the same brazen issue in which the Drug Dosage Table was printed, a British physician named Colin Brewer wrote, "Now some people are . . . worried about appearances. They think that it is a bit undignified to be found by your nearest and dearest with a plastic bag over your head. I think they have a point, but I don't think one should worry about one's appearance at a time like this." Brewer recommended "something about the size of a bag that will fit into a rubbish bin," secured with two or three rubber bands. In a later issue, a reader mentioned that he had performed a dry run on himself and determined that it was easier to put on the rubber bands before the bag than vice versa. He noted that he had demonstrated this technique at his local Hemlock chapter meeting, where "everyone was both amused and impressed."

To understand how truly radical it was to publish explicit information about how to kill oneself, let us remove ourselves momentarily from the hermetic world of the *Hemlock Quarterly* and look at how the mainstream press was handling the question of suicide methods. In 1986, I wrote an article for *Life* about Lois and Paul Martin, terminally ill members of Hemlock who had committed suicide together three years earlier. I knew what drug they had taken, and how much—the dosage had been printed in their *HQ* obituary—but my editors and I decided to omit those details. In fact, in Mrs. Martin's handwritten medication chart, which was reproduced on the first page of the article, we even retouched the name of the drug so as to render it illegible. What exactly were we worried about? I don't know about the editors, but I imagined an elaborate scenario in which a depressed teenager, after stealing the pills from his parents' medicine cabinet, would be found dead with a copy of *Life* on his bedside table, page 71 turned down, paragraph one marked with a yellow Hi-Liter, and my culpable byline exposed to the world's damning scrutiny.

Last November, *The New York Times Magazine* published an article about the assisted suicide of a young, terminally ill woman. The drugs that killed her—forty Nembutals—were not only specified in the article, they were printed in 18-point type on the cover of the magazine. During the seven years that had elapsed between the publication of those two magazine articles, a monumental shift in popular thinking about suicide—about what is taboo and what is not—had taken place. I can think of no other major social issue of the last decade about which public opinion moved so far and so fast. The shift can be largely ascribed to the Hemlock Society's 1991 publication of *Final Exit*, Derek Humphry's nuts-and-bolts suicide manual, and its subsequent ascent to the top of the nonfiction best-seller list. The book received an enormous amount of publicity. Some critics praised its candor; others seemed incredulous that such incendiary material had been allowed into the public domain. None of them mentioned—probably because none of them knew—that *Final Exit*'s most controversial chapters, including its drug chart, had been printed years earlier in the *Hemlock Quarterly*.

According to a recent study published in *The New England Journal of Medicine*, copies of *Final Exit* were found near the bodies of twelve New York City residents who committed suicide in 1992: my nightmare scenario come true. Three other suicides left notes they had copied nearly word for word from page 82 of the book. Of these fifteen *Final Exit* readers, five had psychiatric histories and six not only weren't terminally ill—they weren't ill at all. These deaths received little national attention, although fewer than ten years ago, when suicide manuals published in France and Great Britain similarly facilitated a series of "wrongful deaths," there was a flurry of headlines and lawsuits. I do not believe *Final Exit* should have been suppressed—for better or for worse, America was ready for it—but I find it unsettling that the slackening of suicide's taboos has relieved death not only of its impediments but also, it seems, of its sting.

In the fall of 1989, Derek Humphry left Ann Wickett three weeks after she had undergone a lumpectomy for breast cancer. Two years later, Wickett, who was depressed but not terminally ill, swallowed a fatal dose of barbiturates and left a note for Humphry that read, in part, "There. You got what you wanted." Shortly after Wickett's death, Humphry resigned his dual positions as executive director of the Hemlock Society and editor of the *Hemlock Quarterly*. He maintains that he had wanted to retire for years but could afford to do so only after *Final Exit* made him a rich man, or at least a man who didn't need a pension plan, something Hemlock had never been able to provide.

Thus far Humphry has enjoyed an energetic retirement. Last year he published *Lawful Exit,* a well-researched history of euthanasia-law reform. He also founded a new right-to-die group called the Euthanasia Research and Guidance Organization (ERGO!). Humphry is currently working on the inaugural issue of the *ERGO! Journal,* to be launched this spring, which will provide even more explicit procedural advice than *HQ* did. The kind of articles he plans to run can be previewed in "Self-deliverance from an end-stage terminal illness by use of a plastic bag," a two-page pamphlet available by mail order for $5—$50 for twenty copies—from his home in Junction City, Oregon. In it he spells out for the first time a suicide method that employs only over-the-counter medications rather than prescription barbiturates. The bag is not the backup weapon but the actual instrument of death. Humphry's text, which is printed in boldface, gets right to the point: a thirteen-step death plan so minutely detailed that only a fool could screw up ("11. With two thumbs, hold the elastic bands stretched a few inches from the Adam's apple . . ."). There are even two "photo illustrations" of a simulated suicide, in which a young woman, wearing a dust mask (to prevent the inhalation of plastic into the nostrils) and an ice bag (to reduce heat), fastens a transparent bag around her neck. What could be more user-friendly? What could be more grotesque? After staring for some time at this little pamphlet, I began to wonder if Humphry had *tried* to make it repulsive in order to force the issue of physician aid-in-dying. If you vote no on your state's next euthanasia initiative, he seems to be saying, this is what you will see one day when you open your mother's bedroom door.

The last half-dozen issues of the *Hemlock Quarterly* were edited

by Humphry's former assistant, Kris Larson, who will also edit
TimeLines, *HQ*'s successor. If issues No. 48–53 of *HQ* are any
indication, *TimeLines* (whose very name seems designed to prevent people from knowing they are reading a periodical about
death) will do its best to nudge the camel out of the tent and back
to the desert. Although a few local Hemlock chapters are carrying
on the fight, the national organization, which used to be the
right-to-die movement's vanguard, has drifted to the center in an
effort to distance itself from the radical new organizations—
Compassion in Dying, Oregon Right to Die, ERGO!—that sprang
up after Humphry's resignation. The sanitizing of *HQ* was part of
Hemlock's conservative repositioning. Larson's *HQ*s contained a
great deal of political coverage and not much how-to material.
Kaffeeklatsching was kept to a minimum. Humphry's last issue
contained fourteen letters; Larson's last issue contained one. Instead of sending an occasional personal note to *HQ*, readers were
urged to send their legislators "hundreds and thousands" of "pro-
active postcards," available at nominal cost from Hemlock, featur-
ing the "Good Life/Good Death Logo in glossy eye-catching col-
ors" on one side and plenty of room on the other for "specific
messages advocating particular legislative concerns."

The golden age of M.B. and Mrs. F. was plainly over, but that
didn't mean that the voices of Hemlock's members were entirely
stilled. In a recent article about AIDS and assisted suicide, there
were some memorable offerings from a new Hemlock breed, the
HIV-positive men who now constitute a significant minority of
the society's membership. One man who had facilitated a suicide
commented, "I couldn't do it for just anybody. It would have to be
someone I love. . . . After all, friends help friends, because doctors usually won't." He explained how he had helped:

> When he asked me again I got a big three-quarter bag of heroin. He'd
> never shot up before. I was paranoid about the syringe, and made sure I
> wore gloves to get in and out of his apartment. I shot him up and put his
> hands on the syringe and made it look like an overdose. It took about two
> minutes to really hit him, because heroin builds to a big bang.

Their tastes in suicide methods may be different, but I like to
think that when Mrs. F. read this—if she's still alive herself—she
recognized a Good Samaritan and a kindred spirit.

My back issues of the *Hemlock Quarterly* have been piling up
for more than ten years, and as I reread them all they began to
weigh heavily on me. Death, death, death! My file cabinets

seemed like a charnel house stuffed with rattling bones. I decided that when I finished writing this article I'd throw every last memento mori into the trash.

But my father is eighty-nine. Three years ago he underwent surgery for colon cancer, and last year he lost his vision to retinal necrosis. My mother is seventy-seven. She has arthritis and glaucoma. I kept my back issues. I kept Derek Humphry's plastic-bag pamphlet too, in the same spirit as I have kept—though I have yet to use them—a yellowing collection of newspaper articles about how to refinish a wooden floor, how to plant a window box, how to hang a quilt, and how to set up a saltwater aquarium. You never know when they might come in handy.

℞ FOR DEATH[2]

Death abides with all fanatics, not least because they are so often willing to risk it for their cause. It presses close around Jack Kevorkian, the doctor who has made death his specialty, closer still last week as he returned to the practice that so often had seemed destined to land him in jail. "To go to jail is the ultimate slavery," he told TIME. "If I have lost my freedom, I have lost something more valuable than life. Therefore, continuing life becomes pointless. It's as simple as that." Dramatic self-negation would be a fitting exit for Death's Impresario. But last week Kevorkian made an uncharacteristically humble reappearance with suicide No. 16. By underplaying his hand, he may have found a way to avoid jail—and prolong his controversial crusade.

On May 16, when Kevorkian attended the suicide of Ronald Mansur, a Realtor with bone and lung cancer, he did not bring a video camera, and when it was over, he did not call a press conference. There was no suicide note; there were no relatives looking on and no explanations. Just an anonymous call to 911, telling police where to find the body—in effect, telling the State of Michigan to go to hell.

The last time Kevorkian hauled out his carbon monoxide mask, Michigan's lawmakers decided it was time to shut down his

[2]Article by Nancy Gibbs, staff writer, from *Time* 141:34–39 My 31 '93. Copyright © 1993 by Time Inc. Reprinted with permission.

practice. In February the state declared his specialty a felony punishable by up to four years in jail and a $2,000 fine. Three previous attempts to charge the doctor with murder had failed, and his opponents relished the chance to make something stick. The A.C.L.U. challenged the law, and Kevorkian promised to postpone any further medicide until after the court reached a decision. But apparently he ran out of patience.

Police arrived at a drab cinder-block real-estate office to find Mansur dressed in slippers and wrapped in a white-knit blanket; he was slumped in an easy chair with the telltale mask strapped to his face. A string tied to the middle finger of his left hand was connected to a clip on the tubes running from two cylinders labeled CARBON MONOXIDE. The body was gaunt, the skin yellow-green. For the past few months, Mansur had been too sick to drive and carried a morphine pump around with him to combat the pain. "He was in hell," says longtime friend Donna Cady. "He would cry on the phone." She adds, "I know that when he put that mask on his face he had his finger sticking up in the air to say screw you all for the laws that made me suffer like this."

That would be a gesture familiar to Dr. Kevorkian, who has made defiance of the law a passion second only to suicide. "When the law itself is intrinsically immoral," says Kevorkian's irrepressible mouthpiece, lawyer Geoffrey Fieger, "there is a greater duty to violate the law." Yet this time around Kevorkian merely tiptoed past it. Fieger says the doctor isn't taking any credit for helping a desperate man die. He just wanted to watch.

The police arrested him anyway, but Kevorkian refused to cooperate. "He will not tell us what happened inside the building," says inspector Gerald Stewart, who heads the major-crimes division of the Detroit police department. "We will have to establish that someone did assist in a suicide, and it's kind of difficult." After two hours, during which he watched the Knicks-Hornets play-off game, police released Kevorkian into Fieger's custody.

Kevorkian's new stealth strategy may simply be a means of self-preservation. Indeed, his chances of avoiding prison improved enormously at the end of the week, when Judge Cynthia Stephens, citing a technicality, struck down the Michigan law that threatened to curtail Kevorkian's efforts. Stephens also found that two terminally ill plaintiffs in the A.C.L.U. case had a right to die. She wrote, "This court cannot envisage a more fundamental right than the right to self-determination."

The ruling left Kevorkian's opponents flabbergasted. "If I

were a gambler, I'd bet that Kevorkian will kill someone tomorrow," said local Operation Rescue activist Lynn Mills after hearing
the decision. "He's really out of control."

Over the years Kevorkian has been generous to his adversaries in the church, the press, the medical profession, even the
euthanasia movement. Every time he speaks or writes he hands
them ammunition to dismiss him as a psychopath. "If I were
Satan and I was helping a suffering person end his life, would
that make a difference?" he asks. "Any person who does this is
going to have an image problem." That larger-than-death image
grew with each story of his early experiments transfusing blood
from cadavers to live patients, his paintings of comas and fevers,
his bright-eyed enthusiasm for his "Mercitron" machines. With
his deadly humor and his face stretched tight around his skull, he
has become a walking advertisement for designer death.

The Mansur case, like those that preceded it, captures the
worst fears of opponents of doctor-assisted suicide. By operating
outside the law, they say, doctors like Kevorkian go unregulated,
unsupervised, abiding only by those safeguards they impose on
themselves. They alone make judgments about the patient's state
of mind; about what means, short of death, might relieve the
suffering. They transform the image of the doctor from pure,
emphatic healer to something more ambiguous, even sinister,
whose purpose at the patient's bedside is no longer clear.

But in the eyes even of some who disagree with his methods,
Kevorkian has become the devil that doctors deserve. Arthur
Caplan, director of the University of Minnesota's Center for Bio-
medical Ethics, puts it succinctly. "I'll give him this," he says. "He
tells us exactly where the health-care system stinks." Even some
doctors reluctantly agree. "A significant percent of the American
public sees Kevorkian as a reasonable alternative to modern medicine," says professor George Annas of Boston University's School
of Medicine. "He's a total indictment of the way we treat dying
patients in hospitals and at home. We don't treat them well, and
they know it."

This mistreatment, he says, is a combination of deceit, insen-
sitivity and neglect. "First we don't tell them they are dying. We
do tell them their diagnosis and all the alternative treatments
available. But we don't tell them their prognosis. We tell them
'You have cancer, and you can have surgery, radiation, chemotherapy, or all three together, or even any two.' We don't tell them

that no matter what we do, it's almost certain they are going to die soon."

Worse, he says, doctors ignore their patient's suffering. "Up to 90% of patients die in too much pain. Some doctors actually argue that their patients are going to get addicted. But they can't have thought about it for more than two minutes to say something like that. The vast majority simply don't know how to treat pain, and they don't think it's important. They want to cure the person. Death is still seen as the enemy. And that's what Kevorkian throws in their face. What he says is, 'Some people want death, and I am going to give it to them.'"

Finally, Annas says, "we more or less abandon dying patients. When there is nothing more medicine can offer, we turn them over to the nursing staff, and we don't see them anymore."

Faced with such prospects, is it any wonder Kevorkian has hundreds of letters from people who want him to help them die?

When people are asked how they wish to die, most respond something like this: quickly, painlessly, at home, surrounded by family and friends. Ask them how they expect to die, and the fear emerges: in the hospital, all alone, on a machine, in pain. What Kevorkian claims to offer patients is a chance to control the circumstances of their death—something which, for all the new laws and heightened awareness of recent years, many hospitals and doctors still may fail to do.

Kevorkian knows firsthand about loss of control. "Our mother suffered from cancer," says his sister Margo Janus. "I saw the ravages right up to the end. Her mind was sound, but her body was gone. My brother's option would have been more moral than all the Demerol that they poured into her, to the point that her body was all black and blue from the needle marks. She was in a coma, and she weighed only 70 lbs. Even then I said to the doctor, 'This isn't right, to keep her on IV,' but he shrugged his shoulder and said, 'I'm bound by my oath to do that.'"

When the Supreme Court ruled in 1990 that Nancy Cruzan's parents could remove the feeding tube that was keeping their comatose daughter alive, the Justices affirmed the growing belief that there was no virtue in heroically prolonging life against a patient's wishes. Since then, doctors have invented guidelines, ethicists have organized seminars, and Congress has passed the Patient Self-Determination Act, requiring hospitals to tell people about their right to control their treatment through living wills and powers of attorney. And yet every day in hospitals across the country, patients and their families are learning that, for all the new legal options and heightened awareness, once inside a hospital, there is virtually nothing a patient or a family can do to make dying simple.

When Susan Evans of the University of Pennsylvania's Annenberg School for Communication held focus groups about living wills, she uncovered a deep mistrust between doctors and patients around the subject of dying. Doctors think patients don't want to talk about it; patients think doctors lack the time and training to do so. Some are cynical about doctors' motives. "The longer I am on a machine," one patient said, "the more money they make."

Surveys of doctors themselves show how many are unaware of their patients' options or unwilling to respect them. Many health-care workers knew little about new laws that allowed them to withhold or withdraw machines like respirators and kidney machines or even feeding tubes. Many rejected the idea that once a treatment is started, it can still be dropped, even though the law upholds a patient's right to do so. Though the courts have recognized the right of patients to refuse food and water, 42% of health-care workers rejected that option.

Even when patients go to the trouble of expressing their wishes, the doctor's values may prevail. One study found that in 25 of 71 cases, when patients were moved from nursing homes to hospitals, their living wills never made it onto their hospital charts. "It's easy to say the patient doesn't really understand because he's never been in this situation before and therefore doesn't know what the treatment is all about," says Dr. David Orentlicher, a professor of medicine at Northwestern University. "It's also easy to say to a relative that the patient never really anticipated in his living will this specific situation."

And if the doctor's values don't prevail over the patient's, the families' often will. Given the anguish at the deathbed, it is not surprising that patients and relatives may argue over treatment decisions—or that doctors often side with the family. "The law is designed to give preference to living wills over the wishes of relatives," says Robert Risley, a Los Angeles attorney who drafted the state's initiative to legalize doctor-assisted suicide. "But as a practical matter it throws the health-care provider into a dilemma if there is a conflict."

The fear of litigation also haunts every aspect of treatment. Says Curtis Harris, a specialist in endocrinology and president of the 22,000-member American Academy of Medical Ethics: "I have seen patients that were clearly within the last hours of life and no one could do anything and a white knight son comes in from out of town and says, 'If you don't do everything you can to save her, I'm going to sue your socks off.'" Dr. John Ely, a professor at the University of Iowa College of Medicine says there has never been a successful suit against a physician who gave treatment in accordance with family wishes and against the patient's wishes. "That's because the patients aren't there," he says. "They are either incompetent or they have already died."

Suicide, the unpunishable crime, has always posed a challenge to societies that want to deter it. Under English common law, suicide was a felony punishable by burying the body by a public highway with a stake driven through the heart, to keep the spirit from wandering. It is no longer a crime in the U.S., but assisting in one is illegal in more than 20 states. No one knows how often doctors write the prescription and whisper the recipe for a deadly overdose; but one informal survey of internists last year found that one in five say they have helped cause the death of a patient. Poll after poll shows that as many as half of Americans favor doctors doing so.

Doctors who work with AIDS patients in particular are aware of the underground system that provides the information and the means for suicide. "You have to understand what it is I see," says a Los Angeles doctor, who has prescribed medication that he knew would likely end up killing his patient. "I see people in agony. Most of my patients are pretty sophisticated. They know the exact dosage that will kill them. By God, if someone is dying, far be it from me to say 'Hey, tough it out.'"

But even physicians who spend all their days with the terminally ill are divided over Kevorkian's answer to the problem of pain. Some may respect the patients' decision to kill themselves but draw the line doing it for them. To withdraw treatment merely allows the disease to do the killing. A lethal injection is altogether different. "Medicine is a profession dedicated to healing," the American Medical Association has declared. "Its tools should not be used to kill people."

So far every effort to move the practice out of the legal half-light runs into practical and philosophical trouble. A good law is hard to write, harder still to enforce and easy to abuse. First in Washington and last year in California, voters turned down initiatives that would have legalized assisted suicide if a patient wrote out a "death directive" that was witnessed by at least two people who did not stand to benefit from the death. Doctors would need independent confirmation that a patient had six months or less left—a judgment that is notoriously unreliable. "It's naive to believe it can be regulated," notes ethicist Daniel Callahan of the Hastings Center in Briarcliff Manor, New York. "There's basically no way you can regulate something that takes place in private."

As proof, ethicists point to the world's euthanasia laboratory, the Netherlands, where for almost 20 years the courts have not convicted doctors who assist in suicides at the explicit request of the patient. Last February, the Dutch parliament moved to give doctors the actual right to do so—if they follow strict guidelines for second opinions. Yet a 1991 study found that in one year more than 1,000 Dutch patients who were not capable of giving consent died at their doctors' hands.

That finding fueled the fears of ethicists who believe that legal assisted suicide could become an instrument to meet social or economic goals, even "altruism." For example, people over 65 spend $3\frac{1}{2}$ times as much on health care as younger people. "It would be a terrible burden to put on the disabled, the dying and the weakened elderly, especially at a time when there is enormous pressure to cut medical costs," says Father Richard McCormick, professor of Christian ethics at the University of Notre Dame. "They would constantly ask themselves, 'Should I ask for it, is now the time?'"

As the most prominent "obitiatrist," which is what he would like to call death specialists, Kevorkian has been outspoken about his safeguards. "You act only after it is absolutely justifiable," he insists. "The patient must be mentally competent, the disease incurable." The trouble is that he has trouble meeting his own standards. Over the years, when he has called the doctors and psychiatrists of the people he was working with, they have said they would have nothing to do with him. "Now that's ethical?" he asks. "If doctors won't cooperate, what do you expect me to do? You think I'm going to let the patient suffer because they don't *consult?*"

But if his adversaries are right, one recent case shreds Kevorkian's safety net. In February, Kevorkian assisted in the suicide of Hugh Gale, 70, an emphysema patient who may, at the last minute, have changed his mind. According to one version of the report that Kevorkian wrote, about 45 seconds after putting on the carbon-monoxide mask, Gale became flushed, agitated, saying "Take it off!" The mask was immediately replaced with oxygen, which helped calm him down. "The patient wanted to continue," the report states. "After about 20 minutes, with nasal oxygen continuing, the mask was replaced over his nose and mouth, and he again pulled the clip off the crimped tubing. In about 30 to 35 seconds he again flushed, became agitated with moderate hyperpnea [rapid or deep breathing]; and immediately after saying "Take it off!" once again, he fell into unconsciousness. The mask was then left in place . . . Heartbeat was undetectable about 3 minutes after last breath." Kevorkian's lawyer says the report was an erroneous draft. The prosecutor declined to press murder charges.

In fact, by his own, self-imposed rules, Kevorkian may have gone too far. In an article in the *American Journal of Forensic Psychiatry* last year, Kevorkian sketched a hypothetical example of how a patient, "Wanda Endittal," and her doctors, "Will B. Reddy," "Frieda Blaime" and "Dewey Ledder" should proceed before a suicide: "If in any of her reviews, Wanda manifests *any degree* of ambivalence, hesitancy or outright doubt with regard to her original decision, the entire process is stopped immediately and Wanda is no longer—and can never again be—a candidate for 'medicide' in the state of Michigan."

Kevorkian's opponents also charge that without safeguards and consultations and thorough psychiatric evaluations, patients may seek out suicide not because of their disease, but because of their despair. Recognizing depression in dying patients is hard, since the culture ties the two together. Its symptoms of fatigue, loss of appetite, aches and pains mimic those of advanced cancer. "What Kevorkian's doing is killing people because they're depressed," says James Bopp Jr., an Indiana attorney who is president of the National Legal Center for the Medically Dependent and Disabled. "But depression is curable. He takes absolutely no account of this. He's not qualified to diagnose depression nor is he qualified to treat it."

Kevorkian says that he always tries to talk people who come to him out of killing themselves. But some circumstances, he believes, produce the mental anguish that may justify suicide. "You can't dope up a quadriplegic," he argues. "There's no pain to alleviate, but the anguish in the head is immense, especially after five or 10 years of lying on your back looking up at the ceiling." He says he would love to debate the critics who charge that he is too hasty in deciding who may die. "I will argue with them if they will allow themselves to be strapped to a wheelchair for 72 hours so they can't move, and they are catheterized and they are placed on the toilet and fed and bathed. Then they can sit in a chair and debate with me."

Somewhere between the prospect of a slow death in intensive care and a quick death at the hands of a doctor lies the vast middle ground. It is this middle ground, his critics charge, that Kevorkian in his single-minded focus on death, too often fails to explore. "Our experience says the great majority of the time these people are lonely, isolated and actually in need of better medical care rather than somebody to euthanatize them," says Harris of the American Academy of Medical Ethics.

A few months ago, if asked about Dr. Kevorkian, Solomon Mirin, 81, of Boca Raton, Florida, would have gladly joined in the crusade. "There are too many sick and hurting people in pain, with no quality of life, just waiting to die." But by Jan. 12, his thinking had changed forever. That was the day his wife died.

Just before Christmas, Maxine Mirin began to complain about being tired all the time. On Christmas Day, she was diagnosed with acute myeloid leukemia, and doctors gave her one week to live. She lasted for two. That was all the time it took, Mirin said, to "come 180 degrees in my attitude. I can still intellectualize why people seek out a person like Kevorkian. But I've come to understand that the lives of even the terminally ill are precious and matter, right up to the last second of breath. There is such a thing as dying with grace, dignity, compassion and support, and there are alternatives to the kind of suicide Kevorkian proposes."

Their alternative was a hospice in Atlanta, where the Mirins' nephew lived and where they had already purchased their grave sites. Metro Hospice brought to their nephew's home a wheelchair, hospital bed, special padding, oxygen. They provided care and pain medication during Maxine's last four days. "She was not able to talk, but she was able to hold her hand out to me. She knew I was there and that I loved her and valued her life." Mirin was charged "not even 10¢" for the service; it was all covered by Medicare.

In the past five years, hospitals have recognized the need to set up hospices, but "hospice doctors are considered to be on the margin of medical practice," says Annas. "They are not thought of as real doctors because they don't try to cure people, they just help them die. So many physicians either don't refer patients to hospices or wait until the last week of life before they do it."

Given the ruling last week, Kevorkian seems to have the upper hand—for the moment. "As a practical matter he may now be untouchable unless a new law is passed and then we start all over again," says University of Michigan law professor Yale Kamisar. "He now has the police and prosecutors off-balance." But they would love to take him on. "Every person from the Governor on down has been attacked personally about being a Nazi or a member of a right-wing organization," says Oakland County prosecutor Richard Thompson. "He's basically thumbed his nose at law enforcement, in part because he feels he has public support."

As for the doctor himself, he seems to take some satisfaction in having done his small part. "It's unstoppable," he says. "It may not happen in my lifetime but my opponents are going to lose. There's a lot of human misery out there."

THE OREGON TRAIL TO DEATH[3]

The first "patient" of Dr. Jack Kevorkian's "medicide" was a woman from Portland, Oregon, Janet Adkins, who had been diagnosed with early-stage Alzheimer's. The national headquarters of the Hemlock Society, and the home of Derek Humphry, author of the best-selling book *Final Exit: The Practicalities of Self-Deliverance and Assisted Suicide for the Dying,* are located in Eugene, Oregon. Thus, it comes as little surprise that the state of Oregon will soon join its neighboring states of Washington (1991) and California (1992) in debating and voting on a citizen initiative, Measure 16, to legalize physician-assisted suicide. The expectation of the umbrella Oregon Right to Die Coalition is that the Oregon "Death with Dignity Act" (DDA), unlike its failed predecessors, will appeal to a majority of voters this November. If that scenario occurs, Oregon will have, consistent with its self-

[3]Article by Courtney S. Campbell, associate professor in the Department of Philosophy, Oregon State University at Corvallis, and director of its Program for Ethics, Science, and the Environment. From *Commonweal* 121:9–11 Ag 19 '94. Copyright © 1994 by *Commonweal.* Reprinted with permission.

cultivated image of pioneering moral progressivism, blazed a new trail in providing alternative end-of-life choices for the terminally ill. Whether this trail should be followed is an issue certain to be divisive in our culture for many years to come.

As approved by the Oregon Supreme Court, the DDA asks voters the following: "Shall law allow terminally ill adult Oregon patients voluntary informed choice to obtain physician's prescription for drugs to end life?" While I shall explicate later some of the statutory safeguards and legislative loopholes embedded in this language, it is important initially to recognize the difference in scope between the DDA and the failed Initiative 119 in Washington and Proposition 161 in California. In those referendums, voters were asked to approve "physician aid-in-dying," which included not only assistance in suicide but also active euthanasia, such as lethal injections, by physicians. By contrast, the Oregon DDA restricts the role of a physician to providing the prescription for a drug such as Seconal to end one's life. However, having obtained the prescription, the patient may elect not to use it. Thus the professional's role is deemed by proponents as not morally compromised. Indeed, according to Eli Stutsman, legal counsel for Oregon Right to Die, the DDA simply would "codify existing medical practice" for the terminally ill, thus permitting conduct which is now performed secretly to be performed openly without fear of prosecution (personal correspondence, June 14, 1994).

Stutsman contends that the process of drafting the DDA occurred with three principal constituencies in mind. First, the DDA is intended to advance the interests of patient autonomy by making the right to die "a fundamental civil right." Second, the DDA would ensure that health-care professionals can provide the form of care that best promotes the patient's welfare with guarantees of legal immunity. Finally, the DDA offers to the public a model of "reasonable regulation" of physician assistance-in-suicide with safeguards that the public will understand as "sensible without being onerous." While the public debate is not yet in full swing in Oregon, the efforts to satisfy the interests of these constituencies have so far been successful in dissuading several major political players from expressing opposition to the DDA.

The Oregon counterparts of the political parties and medical associations that opposed the Washington and California initiatives have thus far either endorsed the DDA or adopted a position of "neutrality." A moderate subgroup within the Republican party (The Dorchester Group) endorsed the DDA at its annual conference in February. The traditionally more liberal state Democratic party could not be this specific, although it did affirm in its 1994 platform: "We support the right of terminally ill persons to control their own end-of-life decisions." The bipartisan support of the DDA has certainly delighted proponents: "Death with dignity is an issue that cuts across the political spectrum because it involves personal choice," commented Geoff Sugarman, the executive director of Oregon Right to Die, following the March adoption of the Democratic platform.

Perhaps even more indicative of the state of public discourse are the responses of caregiving associations to the DDA. The Washington Medical Association and the California Medical Association opposed their respective initiatives as "fundamentally inconsistent" with the physician's role as healer, as did the American Medical Association. The Oregon Medical Association (OMA), by contrast, agreed in May to a motion "to neither oppose nor endorse physician-assisted suicide." OMA President Dr. Leigh Dolin publicly discredited concerns about a "slippery slope" impact of the DDA and instead recommended that his fellow physicians listen more to their patients: "We need to hear from the people of Oregon what to do" (Eugene *Register-Guard,* May 2, 1994). It says something profoundly disturbing about the vocational commitments of Oregonian physicians (and perhaps, the medical profession more broadly) that a fundamental matter of medical ethics is presumed to be a choice for the *vox populi.* In what other realm of medicine are physicians so willing to abdicate their power and professional responsibility to public preferences?

A similar scenario has been played out in the context of hospice. The Washington State Hospice Organization and the California Hospice Association each opposed its relevant initiative, as did the National Hospice Organization. The Oregon Hospice Association (OHA) appointed an ethics task force in 1992 to reconsider its 1991 resolution that expressed opposition to assisted suicide and active euthanasia; this ethics task force is currently at a complete impasse, which makes the prospect of a "neutral" position very likely. Some individual hospices have expressed opposition to the DDA, while others have expressed the sentiment that "hospice does what the voters of Oregon want," and have adopted "neutral" policies that will respect personal choice should the DDA pass. Having served on the OHA's ethics task force for some eighteen months ending in March, I find it difficult to see how hospice can affirm neutrality on the DDA without betraying or modifying some fundamental commitments in its traditional caregiving mission, including the value to "neither prolong nor *hasten* death."

These shifts in political and institutional perspective suggest that Oregon Right to Die learned the lessons of failure in Washington and California. It believes that the "sensible safeguards" alluded to by its counsel, Mr. Stutsman, will reassure voters that the DDA will both enhance patient choice and preclude abuse. Using the terminology of the ballot question, let me review and briefly comment on these procedural mechanisms:

• *Terminal illness.* The DDA limits "qualified patients" to persons suffering from an incurable or irreversible health condition that within reasonable medical judgment (made by an attending and a consulting physician) will eventuate in death within six months. It is, however, unlikely that this restriction will remain should the DDA be approved, because it discriminates against persons with similar health conditions who do not fall within the six-month period. The proponents of the DDA deem it important to establish the six-month duration as a precedent that can subsequently be expanded to encompass persons with, for example, early-stage Alzheimer's or HIV disease.

• *Adult Oregon patients.* Proponents have repeatedly emphasized that the DDA would apply only to Oregon residents, and that Oregon need not fear becoming "the suicide destination" of the United States. The problem is that the state's residency requirements are very ambiguous and connected to specific contexts, such as obtaining a driver's license. There is, quite obviously, no such legal precedent to establish residency for assistance-in-suicide, and the DDA itself nowhere defines residency status. Oregon Right to Die contends that since a relationship with a physician licensed to practice in Oregon is also a prerequisite for assistance in suicide, physician licensure provides one necessary check on a quick suicide. However, opponents, organized principally through the umbrella Coalition for Compassionate Care (CCC), contend that this stipulation will become more a drawing card than a safeguard: in the absence of legal precedent, a common law definition of residency status as a "declaration of intent" to become a resident will govern. State legislative counsel have indicated that a court challenge will have to be brought to determine the "common and ordinary meaning" of the term "resident" within the context of assisted suicide (personal correspondence, June 14, 1994), meaning that the questions will not be resolved prior to the November vote.

• *Voluntary informed choice.* The DDA presumes that the diagnosis of terminal illness has no significant influence on the decision-making capacity of a patient. The attending physician is required to inform the patient of the diagnosis, prognosis, potential risks of the prescribed medication; probable result of the prescribed medication; and feasible alternatives, such as comfort care, hospice care, and pain control, as well as the right to rescind a request. The patient is also required to make, fifteen days apart, two oral requests for life-ending medication, as well as one written request which must occur at least forty-eight hours prior to receipt of the medication. These stipulations are deemed to ensure the authenticity and voluntariness of the patient's choice. Moreover, either physician may refer the patient for counseling if he or she suspects the patient is depressed or suffers from impaired judgment. Yet, empirical evidence suggests that depression is often missed or misdiagnosed because the medical training of physicians has focused more on pathologies of the body than those of the mind. The fundamental issue is, then, the appropriate level of trust to vest in physicians regarding their diagnoses of depression or other psychological impairment. The Coalition for Compassionate Care has also raised the prospect of some patients' choices being involuntary because of background social conditions, such as familial pressures, finances, or health-care insurance. Thus, although the DDA would make "coercion" of a patient's choice a Class A felony, the CCC believes that in some circumstances the "right to die" will become a "duty to die."

• *Physicians' prescriptions.* Physicians who participate in assisted suicide must be licensed to practice medicine in Oregon, must verify that the patient's decision is informed, and confirm that the patient is aware he or she can rescind the request. Physicians (or "health care providers") are not obliged, however, to acquiesce in a patient's request; if providers are unable or unwilling to do so, they are required to transfer the relevant medical records of the patient should the patient obtain a new physician.

The claim of proponents that the DDA will simply codify current physician practice must be viewed with a great deal of skepticism for several reasons. It is not at all clear that physician assistance in suicide is already integrated into the dying process; surveys of physicians do indicate a majority would support such a practice if it were legal, but only a minority have actually participated in such an act. Second, even if physician assistance were customary practice, this does not mean the ethical question of whether this practice "ought" to be permissible and customary is answered. Finally, it does not speak highly of the *moral* vocation of the medical profession that its principal concern with the DDA is the question of a physician's legal immunity.

• *Guarding the gatekeepers.* If the safeguards are not as secure as proponents contend, nor as open-ended as opponents maintain, a further issue concerns monitoring of the application of the procedural safeguards. The documenting and reporting requirements of the DDA can be easily circumvented: Not all cases of assisted suicide will be reviewed by the Oregon Health Division (OHD), and reviews of specific cases will not be made a matter of public record. The OHD is required simply to submit an "annual statistical report" to the public.

It is striking that the DDA follows directly on the heels of a major revision in 1993 to Oregon's advance directive law, the Health Care Decisions Act (HCDA). The new law, effective in November 1993, permits patients or designated proxies to forgo all forms of life-prolonging medical treatment as well as "food and water supplied artificially by medical device" under any of the following circumstances: imminent death; permanent unconsciousness; advanced progressive illness; extraordinary suffering. The HCDA also guarantees that patients will receive all necessary and sufficient comfort care and pain control. The legislative history of the HCDA shows that such choices and guarantees were made in part to preclude citizens from resorting to suicide or euthanasia to end their life. Yet, I can attest that a vast majority of Oregon citizens are not aware of the expansive rights they *already* have regarding control over their dying and death, and the DDA itself makes no reference to such rights. Thus, an uninformed citizenry might well think that its only choice in dying is between technological vitalism and assisted suicide.

It must also be said that the DDA initiative imposes its own vision of the good death upon Oregonians. The DDA is quite explicit that assistance in suicide achieves death in "a humane and dignified manner." The moral appeal to dignity, however, is constituted by a need for control and choice over private decisions; community and interdependency are antithetical to this vision of dignity. It is thus not surprising that the DDA encourages, but does not require, family notification of the patient's request to die. Only a very truncated sense of humanity and dignity would not see that the manner and timing of one's dying would be a momentous matter to others in one's community.

The Coalition for Compassionate Care, the principal organized opponents to the DDA, is an umbrella group of religious groups, including the Oregon Catholic Conference, senior citizen associations, and organizations for the disabled. The substantive objections of the CCC are rooted in appeals to the sanctity of human life and concern for vulnerable and marginalized patients in society. Some individuals whose organizations are members of the coalition accept that under very limited circumstances, physician-assisted suicide may be the most morally justifiable and humane course of action to take, but these few situations should not dictate public policy. The DDA is, in any event, seen as unnecessary given the expansive rights of Oregonians under the new advance directive law.

The CCC may take comfort from the comments of an astute observer of Oregon politics, William Lunch of Oregon State University, who has noted that most citizen initiatives fail because the electorate is wary of "change for the unknown." Lunch contends that there are additional factors that will weigh against voter approval of the DDA. First, voters will likely suffer "information fatigue" from confronting as many as eighteen measures on the fall ballot; put another way, the DDA will not "stand out" in the fall run-up to election day. Second, Lunch maintains that the political weight of the Roman Catholic moral tradition and its Oregon constituency will bring a decisive bloc of voters into opposition of the DDA. It is important in this respect to note that in the midst of debate over the 1991 Washington initiative, the bishops of the Oregon Catholic Conference and the Washington State Catholic Conference issued "Living and Dying Well: A Pastoral Letter about the End of Life," which condemned assisted suicide and euthanasia as a denial of personal autonomy and "a lethal, violent, and unacceptable way of terminating care for the infirm."

Although the largest denomination in the state, the Catholic community in Oregon still comprises only 11 percent of the state's population, by itself far smaller than the 17 percent of the state's "unchurched" population. Thus, it is unclear how decisive the Catholic influence, as part of the Coalition for Compassion Care, will actually be in both the public debate and in overall voting patterns. Moreover, public, political, and professional attitudes toward physician-assisted suicide may, as illustrated above, have already changed in advance of the DDA. This is clearly the assumption underlying Oregon Right to Die's view that the DDA will merely codify existing medical practice. If so, voters and others who would follow this Oregon trail to death would be well advised to heed John Updike's words: "Death, once it enters in, leaves its muddy footprints everywhere."

DEATH WITH DIGNITY[4]

Albert Camus wrote in *The Myth of Sisyphus:* "There is only one truly important philosophic problem, and that is suicide." The significance of that sentiment—forcing each of us to a heightened awareness of the elements of human dignity, the sanctity of life, and the very meaning of existence—has perhaps never been more explicit than it is today. For the first time in history, Americans have been asked to decide the crucial question: is it morally permissible (or even admirable) for a human being to end his or her own life or to assist another in shedding this "mortal coil"?

The development of medical technology, pregnant with blessings as well as threats to keep us alive as comatose lumps of flesh, has launched this controversy, commonly labeled as issues of the "right to life." Although a quietly perennial issue, the debate became a public matter in 1974 with the landmark case of Karen Ann Quinlan, a patient whose parents requested the removal of life-sustaining machines. By 1991, 28 states had ruled that patients have the right to refuse life-sustaining treatment. In some locales, the courts indicated merely that competent, mentally alert people could make this judgment; in other states, doctors and relatives are allowed to initiate death when patients cannot request it themselves.

Nine states specifically allow the withdrawal of artificial feeding from patients in a vegetative state, allowing them to starve to death. By 1991, a federal law required that every patient admit-

[4]Article by William McCord, recently deceased, who was an author and a sociologist at the City University of New York. From, *The Humanist* 53:26–29 Ja/F '93. Copyright © 1993 by *The Humanist*. Reprinted with permission.

ted to any hospital for any reason must be asked if they want to plan for their death by filling out a "living will."

Medical "ethicists" have tried to draw a very fine line between withdrawing or withholding treatment and actively assisting others to commit suicide. In practice, this distinction has increasingly lost its meaning. What in fact is the difference between a doctor who starves his patient to death and one who prescribes a dose of seconal with the warning that imbibing a gram will result in death? Most reasonable people today recognize that pulling the plug on a machine or injecting a lethal dose of morphine are both "active" measures that have the same result. What remains in doubt today is who—if anyone—has the right to decide on ending life and what—if any—conditions should limit that decision.

These ambiguities have resulted in a quagmire of contradictory legal opinions. Some states still carry laws on their books punishing the act of suicide as a "crime"; others are silent on the issue; and some punish those who assist in a suicide as "murderers." In Michigan, for example, the State Supreme Court in 1920 upheld the murder conviction of a man who placed poison within reach of his wife, who was dying from multiple sclerosis (*People v. Campbell*). Yet, 63 years later, in a case that never went to trial, a Michigan appellate court ignored this precedent and dismissed a murder charge against a man who gave a gun to a person who was talking of committing suicide and subsequently killed himself.

Dr. Jack Kevorkian exacerbated Michigan's confusion in 1990 when he connected Janet Adkins, a woman suffering from Alzheimer's disease, to a suicide device and watched as she pushed the button. He took the action out of concern for the patient and a desire to force the legal and medical establishments to consider euthanasia as an ethical action. Adkins and her family, anticipating years of degeneration from the disease, requested the procedure. Dr. Kevorkian reported himself to the police immediately after she died. On July 21, 1992, murder charges against Kevorkian were finally dismissed in a Pontiac, Michigan, court; in the meantime, Kevorkian had assisted in several additional suicides.

Voters in the state of Washington decided to put the matter on a democratic ballot. In 1991, citizens of Washington considered a legislative proposition unlike any other ever debated by Americans. Initiative 119 asked: "Shall adult patients who are in a medically terminal condition be permitted to request and receive from a physician aid-in-dying?" The proposition provided that adults could execute a medical directive requesting aid-in-dying only after two physicians certified that they were mentally competent, terminally ill, and had less than six months to live. Two independent witnesses had to certify the patient's decision.

Although public opinion polls indicated that 61 percent of Washingtonians favored the initiative, a majority of voters—54 percent—opposed the measure when it actually came before them. Some, motivated by religious arguments, feared it would undermine the sanctity of life. Others favored euthanasia but questioned whether this proposal had too many loopholes.

Among the issues that disturbed the opponents of the proposition were these: can physicians really know patients' wishes? Can they accurately diagnose and predict how much time is left? Might not patients mistakenly labeled as terminal choose to die needlessly? Would the elderly choose suicide—or even be pushed into death—simply to spare their families' energies, emotions, and pocketbooks?

The Washington vote hardly ended Americans' anguish over the process of dying. A *Boston Globe* poll showed that 64 percent of the public favors letting doctors give lethal injections to the terminally ill; Derek Humphry's *Final Exit,* a handbook on how to commit suicide, achieved bestseller status. And other states have prepared new and improved versions of initiative 119; the first such measure was voted down by Californians in the 1992 elections.

The fact is that the euthanasia issue, especially when linked to the controversy over abortion, has emerged as one of the great debates in turn-of-the-century America; the public must choose between the various "right to life" and "pro-choice" arguments as they apply to death as well as to birth.

Because some Western nations (notably the Netherlands) have long tolerated euthanasia, people on both sides of the issue look to them for enlightenment. The Dutch experience is particularly relevant since the practice of euthanasia is more open and extensive there than any place else in the world. Although Dutch law formally forbids assisted suicide, authorities and doctors have long chosen to ignore the prohibition. According to a government report, 25,300 cases of euthanasia (active or passive) occur each year in the Netherlands; this represents 19.4 percent of all deaths. Of that total, there were 13,691 cases in which an overdose of morphine or the withdrawal of life-sustaining treatment brought about death; and in approximately 39 percent of those deaths, the physicians and families reached the decision to practice euthanasia after the patient's deteriorating state had rendered him or her unconscious and there was no prospect of improvement. In the other cases, the patients themselves reached their decision after rational and prolonged consideration. One study, *Regulating Death* by Carlos S. Gomez, indicates that there are no rigid rules governing the Dutch system. Contrary to American opponents of euthanasia, the Dutch approach has met with wide public approval and has not led to a devaluation of human life *per se*.

Should America follow the Dutch example? In the great debate over this issue—a controversy which is bound to inflame the 1990s—two issues require careful separation. First, does the individual human being have the right to end his or her existence? Second, should society remain aloof from this decision, or should policy establish the ground rules governing the individual, his or her family, and the medical profession?

On the level of the individual, a classic lineage of thinkers from Socrates to Shakespeare to Arthur Koestler have affirmed that humans should have the privilege of selecting their own death—a voluntary, rational, conscious ending chosen not by accident but by lucid free choice. The great Stoic tradition particularly emphasizes that persons have the prerogative of rational suicide—a humane and dignified termination of life chosen courageously and with deliberate self-control.

Following Epictetus, the Stoics sought to rid themselves of "the fetters of the wretched body" and to assert their will "against kings or thieves who, by controlling men's bodies, try to dictate their fate." The Stoics and the Epicureans treasured life; they were not in any sense nay-sayers who wished to escape into a realm of nothingness. As Epicurus wrote: "He is a little man in all respects who has many good reasons for quitting life." And as Epictetus advised his disciples, "Wait upon God. When He gives the signal and releases you from this service, then you shall depart to Him." Nonetheless, the Stoics and the Epicureans believed that the final choice was properly their own—not that of fate or attributable to a supernatural being. Rational persons should make the choice with dignity and fortitude. "Remember," Epictetus wrote, "the door is open. . . . Depart instead of staying to moan."

Similarly, in recent times, Friederich Nietzsche deplored the "unfree, coward's death" that most people, trapped in contemptible conditions at the wrong time and deceived by a slave's morality, must endure. Instead, he celebrated "free death." "From love of life," Nietzsche argued, "one should deserve a different death: free, conscious, without accident, without ambush."

Today, those who contemplate asserting control over suffering and dying contend that the possibility of rational suicide preserves humankind's fragile dignity in the face of brutal circumstances, ironically prolonged by the most modern of medical technology designed to sustain or preserve life. Indeed, they point out that one of humankind's unique and defining attributes is the ability to foresee, to contemplate, and potentially to control our own death; it is this noble quality which sets us apart from all other animals. Rather than degenerating helplessly, the ill person can choose the timing, the setting, and the circumstances of death. He or she may prepare friends and family for the end, make reasonable provisions for the welfare of others, complete worldly duties, and take leave of loved ones in a dignified manner.

By affirming this uniquely human capacity to mediate and mold death, we enhance our threatened autonomy in the face of a remorseless fate. To take the opposite path—as most people do in a mindless submission to the dictates of fate—betrays our highest quality: our capacity for freedom. A death with dignity is a final proof that we are not merely pawns to be swept from the board by an unknown hand. As a courageous assertion of independence and self-control, suicide can serve as an affirmation of our ultimate liberty, our last infusion of meaning into a formless reality.

If rational suicide can serve the cause of human dignity and autonomy, it should also be recognized that such a death may often represent a compassionate act of shielding the person's family, children, and comrades from suffering, needless toll, psychological torture, and even economic catastrophe.

By these considerations—dignity, autonomy, and compassion—a rational suicide may be a noble alternative to enduring the excruciating torment of a final illness. After contemplation, mature persons may choose a death with dignity that affirms their ultimate autonomy and consequently softens the blows that fall upon those they leave behind. Thus, for defenders of rational suicide, as for the ancient Stoics, the image of perfect nobility is the rational person lovingly doing his or her duty to others and meeting death with pride and freedom and courage.

Opponents of the whole concept of a "right" to death appeal

to a wide range of orthodox Jewish and Christian dogmas. They draw, too, on the organizational strength of the right-to-life movement, which portrays euthanasia as one more step toward justifying the elimination of the helpless and the unfit. For them, the biblical command "Thou shalt not kill" applies to oneself as well as others, thus precluding suicide as well as any assistance in suicide. The absolute sanctity of life takes precedence over all other considerations; life must be prolonged regardless of the cost in suffering or debasement.

The sanctity of human life does not depend upon its costs, Cardinal O'Connor of New York argues, and since humans are made in the image of God, the act of suicide necessarily involves deicide. To usurp God's gift of life would be an act of the gravest hubris. The duty of a community of faith is to extend its care to the weakest, sickliest members—not to destroy them. Christians invoke the example of Jesus: "Our Lord healed the sick, raised Lazarus from the dead, gave back sanity to the deranged," Malcolm Muggeridge has pointed out, "but never did he practice or envisage killing as part of the mercy that held possession of his heart."

However, the fact is that the orthodox religious traditions have often sanctioned killing—or even suicide—in the service of some higher goal. For Jews, the mass suicide of the Maccabees in defiance of Roman oppression is now celebrated as a glorious event. For Christians, the other-worldliness of the Pauline tradition sometimes led early converts into an epidemic of suicide. Tertullian describes how entire populations of Christian villages would flock to the Roman pro-consul imploring him to grant them the privilege of martyrdom. Lucian regarded these Christians with scorn; they desired death and gave themselves up to be slain in eager anticipation of eternal salvation. Like Shi'ite martyrs today, some early Christians sought to be slaughtered by their enemies as a sure means of gaining immortality.

Contemporary Christians can dismiss these early tendencies as aberrations and argue that dogmatic justification of some forms of killing—capital punishment and "just wars," for example—are misinterpretations of Jesus' commands. Jesus certainly did not describe martyrdom or suicide as a path to salvation, but, just as surely, he never told humankind to cling to life at all possible costs. His two fundamental commandments—to love God and to love one's neighbor as one's self—do not, in themselves, logically condemn suicide. In fact, a death with dignity, if undertaken in a spirit of compassion for others, could be considered as an ultimate fulfillment of these injunctions. Jesus' poignant acceptance of a crucifixion he could have easily escaped testifies to his conscious willingness to sacrifice his own life for a higher goal.

Regardless of religion, some philosophers—such as Immanual Kant and Albert Schweitzer—have been firm opponents of suicide. Kant knew of the Stoic concern that a noble death for a wise man was "to walk out of this life with an undisturbed mind whenever he liked (as out of a smoke-filled room)." Nonetheless, Kant argued, "man cannot deprive himself of his personhood so long as one speaks of duties, thus so long as he lives." On grounds that are far from clear, Kant thought suicide obliterates morality and degrades humanity since "it eliminates the subject and morality."

Albert Schweitzer, the great proponent of "reverence for life" as a supreme ethical principle, believed that suicide "ignores the melody of the will-to-live, which compels us to face the mystery, the value, the high trust committed to us in life." Schweitzer did not condemn those who relinquish their lives but felt that "we do pity them for having ceased to be in possession of themselves." In truth, Schweitzer did not apply his principle of "reverence for life" very strictly or under all circumstances, since he did not hesitate to eat animal flesh and believed that some wars were justified.

Current opponents of death with dignity believe that society must maintain the taboo against suicide because the right to choose one's own death can quickly become mixed up with the right to "choose" someone else's. Were suicide to be legalized, these people foresee a quick descent into other forms of euthanasia, an unreasonable expansion of the powers of physicians, and an increase in state control over life. Indeed, during the debate over initiative 119, Washingtonians made clear their concern over these possibilities. Many Americans approve of death with dignity for themselves but fear taking the grave step of giving physicians or the state lethal power over others.

When we consider euthanasia as a public policy, we must directly confront these issues. In California and the other states to follow, the clash over current medical and legal arrangements for death will undoubtedly raise such stark problems as these:

• Should the "right" to die extend to those who have already lost the mental capacity to choose for themselves? Opponents of rational suicide believe that allowing such an option would open the door to eliminating everyone deemed "unfit." To avoid reviving the nightmare of Nazism, proponents of euthanasia must clearly affirm the principle of autonomy: the conscious, free, and consenting person must make the original choice of terminating life. "Living wills" and the protections afforded by initiative 119 must guarantee that the patient voluntarily and intentionally requested assistance in death before an incapacitating illness or coma occurred. Such a provision would bar the door to experiments in eugenics and would, in fact, impose stricter restrictions on the "right to die" than now exist in many states.

• Should persons afflicted with serious conditions but who are not near death be allowed to end their lives? Proponents contend that people who are still able to choose but who are physically helpless (such as paraplegics) and those who are diagnosed as being on the brink of an inexorable decline (such as Alzheimer patients) should be allowed to consider suicide as a viable option. Opponents contend that such a concession would open the door for the mentally unstable, the temporarily depressed, or the immature to end their lives prematurely.

Clearly, people who pass through a period of clinical depression often entertain the idea of suicide but reject it when they are properly treated. Similarly, a large number of American teenagers—roughly one in 12 high-school students (grades nine to 12)—say that they have tried to commit suicide at least once. (In fact, the rate of actual suicide is much lower than for the elderly and those with degenerative diseases.) Nonetheless, the fact remains that temporarily dejected people—for example, teenagers who have separated from someone they love—or even revengeful persons do commit suicide. While it will be impossible to prevent all of these deaths, an argument for the right to die with dignity does not mean that society would make it easy for the deranged, irrational person to end life capriciously.

To guard against this, public policy should provide that only mature, mentally competent adults with acceptable reasons are allowed to make the decision—and then only after a certain waiting period. Before a person's request for assistance in dying is approved by a public body, it would be wise to have psychologists or psychiatrists consult with the patient and explore all of the options open to that person. While such an approach would screen out some disturbed, impetuous, harassed, or temporarily dejected patients, it would allow people who rationally anticipate a life of misery to choose death with dignity.

Some other issues to consider:

• Should physicians be in charge of the actual death? Their oath requires them to prolong life; if they shorten it, this sends an ambiguous message to the society. Thus, in general, physicians should not be directly involved in ending life—certainly less so than they are now. In the termination of feeding or, indeed, in capital punishment, Kevorkian has suggested that doctors should not use his suicide machine; instead, consistent with the principles of autonomy and dignity, the patients themselves (or trusted relatives) must take the final action. Kevorkian envisions suicide clinics administered by paramedical workers who would be salaried so that there would be no profit motive involved.

• What if doctors make a mistake? Inevitably, doctors may miscalculate their diagnoses or a "miracle" may extend the life of a hopeless patient. Conceivably, a new treatment could result in unexpected cures (although the lag between the discovery of a beneficial therapy and its application is seldom less than a year). This is unquestionably one of the great risks of medical practice, and it suggests again that the role of the physician should be minimized; the doctor should be an expert counselor but not the person who controls or executes the decision. The burden of the choice must be born by the patient; the exercise of an individual's autonomy should be that person's sole responsibility.

• If rational suicide were freely and broadly allowed, would the elderly, terminally ill, or even seriously ill choose it simply to spare their families' lives and pocketbooks? Possibly. Like the terminally ill in pre-modern Eskimo society, patients might well act out of consideration and compassion for their families. Such self-sacrifice should not be condemned as necessarily evil, but it must not be undertaken lightly. As in other cases, a frank, open, and loving consultation between patient and family should precede any action.

• Is there a grisly possibility that someone—even a person's own family—could push that person into suicide against his or her will? Is it possible that a murder could be hidden as suicide? This could occur—as indeed it already does. The Dutch experience, however, indicates that the legitimation of rational suicide does not *increase* this possibility. With the safeguards proposed even in initiative 119, it seems reasonable to suppose that the chances of murder masked as suicide would actually be decreased.

• Doesn't the hospice movement offer a better alternative than rational suicide? It certainly provides an important alternative and a humane mode of coping with death under circumstances of relatively little pain. However, whether it is better to perish slowly, benumbed by morphine cocktails, or to be allowed to choose the mode, manner, and timing of one's death is, in the opinion of this author, a matter best left to individual discretion.

The obstacles to a public policy of euthanasia are admittedly formidable, but they are not insurmountable. A failure to decide these issues because of personal or social anguish over "contemplating the unthinkable" will continue to condemn many people to humiliating debility, pointless suffering, and perhaps meaningless "final exits." In contrast, sensible provisions for rational suicide—governed by the principles of autonomy, dignity, and compassion—offer humankind the possibility of ending a life that was so acceptable that it required no further deeds or days.

IV. KEVORKIAN'S CRITICS

EDITOR'S INTRODUCTION

Dr. Jack Kevorkian has provoked strong opposition since beginning to assist the terminally ill to die in 1990. The religious right, for example, contends that assisted suicide, like abortion, violates the natural order and sanctity of life. The first article, by Joseph P. Shapiro, from *U.S. News & World Report,* maintains that physician-assisted suicide obscures certain critical issues. Medical and social service breakthroughs, he claims, can ease the pain of dying and relieve the financial burden of costly care. Moreover, a patient's wish to die may result from depression, which if treated may give him or her quite a different outlook.

Jeanne Guillemin, however, is critical of the present medical system. In her article from *Society,* she argues that hospitals are too depersonalized and treatment for the dying too expensive for most. Guillemin adds that hospice care, once described as a more humane alternative to dying in a hospital, provides only minimal supplies and services. She, however, maintains that Dr. Kevorkian's solution is not the answer. Next, Peter J. Bernardi's *America* article explains the Catholic Church's position against physician-assisted suicide, asserting that life is a gift from God that human beings cannot choose to end. Lastly, writing for *Society,* Norman K. Denzin contends that Kevorkian's answer only provides an illusion of control over terminal illness. He also disagrees with Kevorkian's conclusion that euthanasia is positive inasmuch as vital organs are donated to save lives, for this reduces the human body to commodities or objects of exchange. Denzin concludes with a vision of funeral homes in which rows of death machines are plugged into dying bodies. As family members look on, their loved ones drift off into death, and behind closed doors their bodies are taken apart to be experimented on.

DEATH ON TRIAL[1]

There have been no miracles, no cures. But Donna White no longer plots her own suicide. Death will come any day now from the coronary artery disease that already requires the 37-year-old woman to breathe from an oxygen machine and inject herself with morphine. When White got sick, she knew that Dr. Jack Kevorkian was helping people like her end their lives. But like most Americans, she had never heard of hospice care or the medical advances that could ease her terrible pain. Instead, she bought the Hemlock Society's bestselling suicide guide, *Final Exit,* and looked for a doctor who would provide lethal drugs.

For many, the public dialogue over death and dying has become badly distorted. That is clear when a how-to-kill-yourself guide that weighs the relative merits of cyanide vs. car exhaust sells a half-million copies and a quirky pathologist becomes an icon of compassion for helping 20 frightened people end their lives. Too often, death is viewed as inevitably painful, suicide is seen as an act of logic and courage and euthanasia is treated as a civil right.

But a growing number of doctors and bioethicists are challenging these attitudes. They say the public fascination with Kevorkian, who is scheduled to go on trial this week for violating Michigan's law against assisted suicide, obscures the truly important story about dying: that medical and social service breakthroughs can take the pain and financial ruin out of most deaths. In the words of Dr. Joanne Lynn, a noted specialist in aging and dying, "It is an outrage for us to seriously discuss killing the sufferer rather than relieving the suffering."

Without doubt, modern dying has become fearsome. Doctors now possess the technology to forestall natural death almost indefinitely. Too often, the terminally ill suffer needless pain and are kept alive without real hope, as families hold a harrowing deathwatch. Both Lynn and Kevorkian start with the same question: How can we help people die in comfort and with control

[1]Article by Joseph P. Shapiro, staff writer, from *U.S. News & World Report* 116:31+ Ap 25 '94. Copyright © 1994 by *U.S. News & World Report*. Reprinted with permission.

over their final days? Kevorkian's answer is to allow broad access to euthanasia; Lynn's is to apply ever growing knowledge about palliative care. The problem, says University of Minnesota bio-ethicist Arthur Caplan, is that the ways to help people die in comfort—thorough health coverage, good hospice and home care and aggressive pain control—"have taken a back seat to the movement to legalize euthanasia."

Few issues are as personal or divisive as euthanasia. The right-to-die movement started some 20 years ago, in response to the drawn-out dying of comatose Karen Ann Quinlan. At issue was the right of patients to refuse unhelpful treatments. Now, all 50 states and the District of Columbia have enacted laws to allow the signing of living wills, advance medical directives or both. As a result, passive euthanasia—the act of withholding or withdrawing life-sustaining technology, like a feeding tube or respirator—is now common practice.

The new frontier is active euthanasia, in which a doctor acts deliberately to cause early death. Americans' ambivalence about death making is clear in Michigan's love-him, hate-him response to Kevorkian, who has forced the debate over the subject. He faces trial for breaking a 14-month-old ban on assisting in a suicide—a law aimed expressly at stopping him. Yet a state appeals court is considering multiple challenges of the law's consti-tutionality, and rulings so far have backed Kevorkian. He has further support from key members of a citizens committee ap-pointed by the state Legislature, who are urging that Michigan not only repeal the current ban but become the first place in the world to legalize physician-assisted suicide. Similarly, Oregon may vote on an assisted-suicide resolution in November, and a court suit seeks to legalize assisted suicides in Washington State.

Many doctors and ethicists warn that although physician-assisted suicide may seem compassionate, there are dangers aplenty. Among them:

• **Danger 1: Losing Focus.** When Donna White first got sick, her pain cut so deep that she wished for pills, poison, starvation, Kevorkian—anything to end her torment. In bed at night, she would thumb through *Final Exit*, memorizing instructions about deadly drug dosages and how to avoid an autopsy. Like most facing death, White had three fears: she didn't want to die in pain, alone or at great financial and emotional cost to her family. Her best friend agreed to help her end her life—and memorized the book's tips to avoid prosecution—while White searched for a doctor to provide the lethal pills.

Instead, like 250,000 other terminally ill Americans each year, White found hospice care—and some entirely different solutions. A hospice nurse who was a specialist in pain relief joined with White's doctor to find a more effective combination of drugs and taught White how to control the amount she used. Says White, "Once they got my pain under control, I started thinking with my heart." Next, hospice staff built a support network of home aides, therapists and counselors. Since in-home hospice care runs about $80 a day, compared with $1,000 a day or more for a hospital intensive care unit, White was reassured that she would not be "a financial burden on [her] family." A social worker also helped White and her daughter, Carrie, discuss the coming death—and today White's goal is to see Carrie's high school graduation in May.

"Almost everybody who gets a terminal diagnosis goes through a momentary period where they think of suicide," says Maggie Callanan, co-author of *Final Gifts* and one of the hospice nurses who first helped White. Yet few request assistance in dying. Of the more than 1,000 patients Callanan has counseled, only 10 ever asked about suicide, and only one followed through. The numbers would jump, Callanan fears, if assisted suicide were readily available.

The case of Thomas Hyde may support her point. Kevorkian is accused of helping Hyde commit suicide, even providing the carbon monoxide that killed him. Videotapes at the Michigan trial will show that it was the 30-year-old ex-construction worker who sought out the suicide doctor. Hyde's girlfriend, Heidi Fernandez, will testify that Hyde hated the amyotrophic lateral sclerosis that left him unable to lift their infant daughter or hold a hammer. The illness had struck quickly—within a year Hyde could no longer walk or speak clearly—and he knew he faced a difficult death.

What is almost certain to be lost at Kevorkian's trial is the rarity of Hyde's choice. In a survey of 89 people with ALS even more advanced than Hyde's, Dr. John Bach of the New Jersey Medical School found that only two said they regretted being alive or dependent on a respirator. Exceptional cases like Hyde's spread misconceptions that it is logical for people with such illnesses to want death, Bach argues, and that the most compassionate thing society can do is provide a means for ending their lives.

Among those who are most susceptible to such beliefs, Bach argues, are doctors, who almost always underestimate their patients' desire to live. In another study, Bach asked 600 ventilator-dependent adults with debilitating neuromuscular conditions whether they were satisfied with their "life as a whole," and fully 82 percent responded positively. Only 24 percent of doctors and nurses predicted such positive answers. "Doctors assume that because they wouldn't want to be disabled themselves, their patients wouldn't either and that they are better off dying," says Bach.

Almost no one *has* to die in pain, says Dr. Ronald Blum of New York University's Kaplan Cancer Center. That some still do is a result of poor medical practice, he says. One new survey found that 42 percent of all patients with metastatic cancer who had pain were undermedicated. The cause: Doctors simply do not know how to use drugs effectively; they fear, falsely, that they will turn patients into addicts or knock them into drug-induced stupors. And they worry about regulatory scrutiny. Still, only 31 percent of dying patients even need a painkiller the day before they die, according to another study. And new drugs and techniques—including letting patients decide for themselves when to increase medicines—are improving pain management. Nearly 100 percent of cancer pain is controllable, specialists say, although pain research for AIDS and other chronic illnesses remains less advanced.

• **Danger 2: Physicians as Killers.** Doctors shall not kill. That's the foremost rule of medicine, dating back 2,500 years to the teachings of the Greek physician Hippocrates. That healing is a physician's priority has served society well, argues University of Chicago physician-ethicist Leon Kass, because it allows patients to trust their doctors. "Physicians are always tired by patients slipping or not getting better," says Kass. "Once they think of death as a treatment option, then physicians simply give in to their weaknesses."

For proof, Kass points to the Netherlands. An informal, de facto arrangement with prosecutors some 20 years ago allows physicians there to help patients die and avoid litigation, as long as certain safeguards are followed. The patient, for example, has to be terminally ill, in considerable pain and mentally competent and must repeatedly express a wish to die. The system is popular with the Dutch and a model for euthanasia's supporters around the world.

But there is a dark side to the Dutch practice. In slightly more than half of euthanasia cases, for instance, doctors kill *without the patients' knowledge or consent.* That figure comes from the government's own pro-euthanasia report in 1991, which noted that there had been 2,300 cases of doctors killing patients upon request in the preceding year and an additional 400 in which doctors provided pills or other means for suicide. An additional 1,040 people were killed by doctors who acted on their own, without a request from the patient. Of these, 72 percent had never indicated they wanted their lives terminated. Further, notes Rita Marker of the International Anti-Euthanasia Task Force, in 8,100 deaths not reported as euthanasia, doctors deliberately gave overdoses of drugs—not primarily to relieve pain but to bring death. And 4,941 of these occurred without the patient's consent.

Dutch doctors defend their actions by saying they did what they believed a patient or his family would have wanted. But in 45 percent of cases of involuntary euthanasia in hospitals, doctors didn't even consult family members.

Dutch patients now have less control over the way they die, argues Richard Fenigsen, a retired Dutch physician and euthanasia opponent. "The euthanasia movement actually promised liberation by death from the power of medicine," he says. Instead, "the power of doctors increased immensely. Doctors determine how euthanasia is practiced, they establish the diagnosis, they inform the patient if they want, they decide whether to report it to the authorities—and most cases are not reported."

Despite protests by Fenigsen and others, in January a new law took effect that further liberalized the Dutch practice. For the first time, involuntary euthanasia is officially permitted if a doctor can argue it is what the patient would have wanted. "The new law only formalizes a practice that has been accepted for 20 years," says Johan Legemaate of the Royal Dutch Medical Association. "Doctors do not perform euthanasia for pleasure; they do it to relieve suffering."

• **Danger 3: The Slippery Slope.** American supporters of euthanasia say questionable Dutch practices could be avoided here. In our more litigious society, they argue, doctors would fear overstepping legal safeguards. One commonly proposed safeguard is that a patient would qualify for suicide help only if he were in the last six months of life and in intractable pain. But, as Kevorkian's lawyer, Geoffrey Fieger, notes, no doctor can say with certainty when a patient has six months to live. And once a patient in pain is allowed to die, isn't it then immoral to deny the same right to someone in terrible pain who faces a life of torment? Further, if competent people can seek death, then how can the same option be denied to sick babies, adults in comas or others unable to speak for themselves?

Facing these same logical challenges, the Dutch expanded euthanasia dramatically. The Dutch Pediatric Association has issued instructions allowing euthanasia for babies who are not terminally ill but simply face chronic sickness or mental retardation. The rules let doctors decide whether treatment is in "the best interests" of the baby, says Dr. Pieter Sauer, co-author of the instructions.

Then there's the case of Hille Hasscher. The 50-year-old Dutch woman was not terminally ill—just deeply depressed. She had faced a bitter divorce and the deaths of her two sons, one by cancer and the other by suicide. She, too, had tried to commit suicide. When she threatened it again, her psychiatrist prescribed a lethal potion of 20 barbiturates, which she used in 1991 to kill herself. Last April, a court acquitted the psychiatrist, ruling that in a society that allows the self-sacrifice of those in physical pain, it was suitable for a doctor to help someone in unbearable emotional misery.

• **Danger 4: Blurring Suicide's Line.** Coroners report a newly popular method of suicide almost never seen before 1991: asphyxiation by plastic bag. Readers of *Final Exit* will recognize this as a recommended method of death. The book's jacket claims that it "is intended to be read by a mature adult who is suffering from a terminal illness and is considering the option of rational suicide if and when suffering becomes unbearable." But researchers have found that new suicide options are mostly used not by the terminally ill but by the treatably depressed—including teens (more than half a million of whom attempt suicide each year) and the elderly (who have the fastest-rising suicide rates). In New York City, the number of suicides by plastic bag jumped from nine to 40 in the year *Final Exit* was published, and researchers concluded that "most persons exposed to *Final Exit* were not terminally ill."

Although supporters of euthanasia talk about "rational suicide," experts in suicide like psychiatrist Yeates Conwell say there is rarely, if ever, such a case. In one study of 44 end-stage cancer patients co-authored by Conwell, only three had considered suicide, and each of them had a severe clinical depression.

What makes an expanded right to suicide so dangerous, Conwell contends, is that physicians rarely spot depression in patients, particularly older ones. Ironically, he says, the depression typical of the elderly and the terminally ill is easily treatable, unlike the psychotic disorders more common in younger people who commit suicide. Dr. David Clark, a suicidologist, reports that the terminally ill are only slightly more likely than other Americans to commit suicide. Those with terminal illnesses make up 1.4 percent of the population and only 2 to 4 percent of suicides.

• **Danger 5: Making It a Duty to Die.** To be fair to President Clinton, it was NBC's Tom Brokaw, in a question, who first put living wills in the context of saving money. Nonetheless, the president's answer was jarring. There are "a lot of extra costs" in medical care at the end of life, and getting more Americans to sign living wills is "one way to weed some of them out," Clinton said last November.

But the point of a living will is to give the signer autonomy over medical treatment—not a way to die early and save money for a fiscally strapped government. Clinton's answer raised an issue rarely spoken but highly feared: that a right to die can easily become a "duty to die" for the elderly, the sick, the poor and others devalued by society.

The American Medical Association last December adopted a strong anti-euthanasia statement. Dr. Lonnie Bristow, chairman of the AMA's board of trustees, said the group was moved mostly by fear of a coming press for cost containment. "It is a gross conflict of interest for a physician to treat an individual patient and have to worry about the needs of society" for cost cutting, says Bristow.

The current debate in the Netherlands over health care rationing gives credence to Bristow's pessimism. It was recently played out in a macabre six-part TV show called "A Matter of Life or Death." Co-financed by the Dutch Ministry of Health, the show pitted patients in need of lifesaving care against each other. In one episode, two women described their spreading cancers before the studio audience voted on which one should get an expensive drug. Doctors made the actual treatment decisions for the women, but Fons Dekkers of the Dutch Patients Federation, an anti-euthanasia group, called the program "almost immoral."

Polls show it is the young and healthy—not the old and sick, as is widely assumed—who clamor for a right to die. One Harvard study showed that 79 percent of those ages 18 to 34 believe a physician should be allowed to give lethal injections to the terminally ill, but only 53 percent of older Americans agree. Says Dr. Judith Ahronheim of New York's Mount Sinai Hospital: "When my patients get sick or very old, they have a different view: they want to live."

Others who are devalued by society or who lack access to health care also express suspicion of euthanasia. The *Detroit Free Press,* for example, found that only 22 percent of blacks in Michigan said they envision choosing assisted suicide, compared with 53 percent of whites.

That poll found a deep split among women, too. Some fear that because women often play the role of caretaker, they will most feel pressure to take an easy death rather than be a burden on families. But younger, particularly college-educated, women tend to support assisted suicide, often seeing euthanasia as comparable to a woman's right—based on privacy and self-determination—to choose abortion. It is a parallel argued by both Kevorkian and abortion-rights leaders. Planned Parenthood's Pamela Maraldo proclaims: "Choice is choice." However, some civil libertarians, like University of Michigan Law School Prof. Yale Kamisar, argue that the abortion and euthanasia debates are not the same. Most important, notes Kamisar, courts have ruled that abortion is legal because a fetus is not a person. Still, euthanasia's few effective opponents—like the Roman Catholic Church—tend also to oppose abortion.

Such debate shows that little is clear cut about physician-assisted suicide. When proposals to legalize it were put before voters in Washington and California, early polls showed broad support, but the measures were ultimately rejected. Americans there, as elsewhere, have found that the more they consider euthanasia, the more difficult it becomes to resolve its dangers.

PLANNING TO DIE[2]

Thirty years ago, in *The American Way of Dying,* Jessica Mitford roundly criticized Americans for their obsessive denial of death

[2]Article by Jeanne Guillemin, professor of sociology at Boston College, from *Society* 29:29–33 Jl/Ag '92. Copyright © 1992 by *Society.* Reprinted with permission.

and their equally obsessive fixation on immortality. To the puritanical American sensibility, a miasma of shame surrounds the event of death. The quicker one died and the less the family and community were troubled, the better. Funeral directors, a uniquely American profession, assumed all responsibility for the corpse, including its embalmed, cosmetic display and its rapid dispatch to the cemetery or to the crematorium. Denial of death was also the theme of Philippe Ariès's work *Western Attitudes Toward Death* (1974). He credits early twentieth-century America with the invention of the modern attitude toward mortality. Death, once so banal a presence that Renaissance markets were held in graveyards and so communal that relatives and friends crowded the bedchambers of the dying, lost its tame aspect. Under the influence of urban industrialization, it became detached from domestic traditions, not the least of which was a religious understanding of the appropriateness and even the banality of the self's demise. In our times, Ariès argues, death became wild and obscene because we cherish an individualism that cannot be relinquished without extreme anguish. As with sex, death was not to be talked about in front of children or in polite company.

Today the American public is confronting mortality in ways that were unthinkable when Mitford was writing and improbable even to Ariès. The emphasis now is on rational planning for one's death that goes far beyond buying a burial plot. Topics such as traversing the emotional stages of dying, how to compose a living will to instruct final medical decisions, and the merits of rational suicide are ordinary fare on television and radio talk shows and in popular magazines. The head of the Hemlock Society, Derek Humphry, has a bestseller in *Final Exit,* a how-to book on "happy death." Jack Kevorkian, another book author, has gained notoriety for his "mercitron" devices, recently used by three women to end their lives. Despite his subsequent indictment for homicide, the public is far from outraged by the idea of physician-assisted suicide. In 1991, the state of Washington gained national attention with a popular referendum on the issue. The voting public there ultimately balked at granting it legal status, but polls had already revealed widespread support for the option of medically supervised suicide. In 1992, the state of New Hampshire initiated the nation's first legislation that would authorize physicians to write prescriptions to hasten the death of terminally ill patients.

This new frankness concerning death is due in part to changing demographics. The population of the United States has aged, with more people than ever living out a seventy-two year life span. Many are surviving decades beyond it. Perhaps aging alone would shift any society's focus to the end of life. Yet death itself has become unexpectedly familiar because of the AIDS epidemic, which has brought grief to hundreds of thousands of young victims, their families, and friends. Add to this the fact that the United States has the highest homicide rate of any industrialized country, with a disproportionate number of casualties among young minority males, and the difficulties of denying death and its repercussions become clear. Old or young, one thinks, "This could be me."

Still, death is far from tamed; it is now newly wild and familiar. The current discussion of how to die gives evidence of terrible fears that those final circumstances are beyond one's control. In a culture that prizes individual autonomy, there is a no more degrading scenario than the gradual diminution of physical and mental powers, the prolonged and painful helplessness, with mental lapses preceding and even obscuring the experience of dying. American anxiety about dying centers on how the individual can avoid dependence. Unfortunately, the two environments where death is likely to happen are poorly prepared to reduce this anxiety and are, in fact, increasing it. Neither the hospital, where 80 percent of Americans die, nor the home, where growing numbers of patients are being cared for, can be counted on to alleviate fears about death as a scenario of degradation.

Hospital Care and Uncare

In pondering the phenomenon of shameful death ("la mort inversée"), Ariès sees the modern hospital as the environment where depersonalized efficiency and order quell the fears of the dying. As a cultural instrument of repression, the hospital guarantees that the graceless, physically repulsive facts of expiration are hidden from view and that the emotional climate at the bedside is restrained. The sheets are clean, the meals regular, and the staff professional. Replacing family and friends is the hospital team, led by the physician. "They are," wrote Ariès, "the masters of death—of the moment as well as of the circumstances. . . ."

In the last two decades, hospital-based medicine has undergone radical changes and Americans have largely lost confidence in its protective guarantees, as chill and repressive as they have been. Hospital organization, once able to guarantee benign order for both birth and death, has been altered not with reference to the social or spiritual needs of patients, but in reaction to market incentives that favor large hospitals selling progressive medicine. The hospitals that survived the fierce competition of the 1980s did so by heavy investment in new and experimental technologies and by the build-up of centralized facilities offering a profitable mixture of specialized and acute care services. Small community hospitals closed by the hundreds. Public hospitals, burdened with welfare patients, are foundering. Private mega-hospital chains, like Humana, thrive because they serve only privately insured patients.

Far from being beneficent institutions, most hospitals today are businesses that serve clients. Linked to proliferating technological options and required to support high-priced professionals, their main incentive is to maximize returns on their investments. They are only unlucky if they do not. Cost control measures to cap procedure charges, such as Diagnostic Related Groups (D.R.G.'s), have merely succeeded in moving patients more quickly out of their hospital beds to make room for more. Costs for hospital medicine and services continue to rise and inflate health insurance coverage, which growing numbers of Americans cannot afford.

The progressive technologies being marketed through American hospitals fall into two categories. Both affect how we die. One kind addresses the diseases of the growing numbers of patients fortunate enough to survive past youth, at which point they become vulnerable to cardiac disease, cancer, stroke, kidney and liver failure. When Aaron Wildavsky coined the phrase, "doing better and feeling worse," in reference to modern American health care, he aptly summarized its major problem. The important determinants of health and illness—life style, genetics, and the environment—are outside the scope of medicine. Its principal technologies, geared toward an aging clientèle, must be of the patch-and-mend variety, lacking the "magic bullet" efficiency of penicillin and sulfa drugs. Success with these "half-way technologies," as Lewis Thomas called them, is difficult and uncertain. Very sick patients do much more than lose faith in medicine. They take it on, they wrestle with it, and often they feel defeated by it. They are not just disappointed consumers. They engage their bodies and souls in a battle for life.

The role of the physician in treating the very sick patient is problematic, in part because doctors are only apparently disinterested in advising about medical treatment options. Many patients fail to understand that physicians like car dealers, will promote their products, if asked. Not that physicians are necessarily driven by profit motives, but they are integrated into the hospital reward system, now heavily invested in high-technology resources—machines, laboratories, consultants—that must be used to get a return. Perhaps unwittingly, physicians often inform seriously ill patients about therapy in ways that encourages it. The use of statistical odds, for example, is a commonplace, as when a doctor refers to scientific studies to inform a patient about survival rates for cancer, using surgery or drugs or some combination of both. When cancer or any other disease is in an advanced stage, this tactic is little better than offering a lottery ticket to someone who is destitute. What even educated patients often do not know is that many clinical studies are poorly executed—without controls and on small samples—and yield only the most tentative results. Or, if they are well conceived and implemented, the patients researched may share none or few of the characteristics— age, gender, medical history, and so on—of the patient being informed. There is little or nothing in their training that prepares physicians to develop a posture of integrity and more genuine disinterest or new words of counsel for the seriously ill who should perhaps not venture any therapeutic course.

For a very sick patient, surgery, chemotherapy, or organ transplant might work. Then again, it might not. It will certainly be a physical and emotional ordeal, causing pain that is especially alienating because it is impossible to know whether it is part of recuperation or a sign of further degeneration. The patient cannot know, nor can the therapist, until test results come back. Even then, many therapies require years of monitoring, especially in the case of cancer, during which one simply does not know if a true cure has been effected. Starting with Susan Sontag's *Illness As Metaphor* to the essay on resisting chemotherapy by the anthropologist Susan DiGiacomo, the patient-as-survivor literature constitutes a searing criticism of how physicians mishandle patients confronting death.

The really bad news is that medical technology can offer multiple sequential therapeutic options for the same fatal disease. This creates uncertainty and uncertainty in medicine, as Wildavsky and others have noted, is often resolved by doing more. If drugs and surgery fail, other drugs or more surgery are substituted. The more advanced the disease, the more the desperate patient will value inclusion in an experimental trial of some new therapy, whereby she or he is diminished to a statistic and risks more physical devastation. This way of progressing toward death—by hopes raised and dashed, by technological assaults on the body, followed by periods of incomplete and uncertain recuperation—is, of course, not the road traversed by people who are cured. Many people overcome blocked arteries, for example, or cancer because the therapy works. But subjection to experimental medicine is the pathway of everyone's last cure. No matter what the patient's age or how advanced the disease, or even if it is considered incurable, the options for more tests and treatment exist, in refined or experimental form, appropriate or inappropriate, as the physician advises.

The intensive care unit [I.C.U.] is the other important kind of technology that hospitals market. It has revolutionized the way Americans die, but not for the better. The concept of high-technology life support took hold in the early 1970s in response to a perceived need, public and professional, for emergency medical services. The argument for emergency medical units was and is based on the reduction of waste in human lives. Immediate aggressive intervention, not unlike that of a M.A.S.H. unit, would save victims of accidents, of heart attack and stroke, as well as premature infants, and post-operative patients. The key was vigorously sustained intervention with the maximum resources of a large central hospital. Emergency and intensive care facilities, costing billions of dollars, became part of the expansion of central hospitals throughout the 1970s and 1980s. Patients *in extremis* are always in good supply and treating them quickly in high-use beds has often helped hospitals underwrite less profitable services. Such heavy investment in acute care emphatically denied a preventive and more cost-efficient approach to health problems and to the general social problem of death by violence. Nor did emergency care enthusiasts predict that many whose lives were saved would not be able to resume normal lives or even a conscious existence, and would be passed off to chronic care facilities or to their families.

Even less concern is being expressed for the I.C.U. patient's experience of having to live attached to machines or dying that way. From the perspective of the conscious patient, experiencing what it means to be "worked on" by teams of strangers, to be coded for resuscitation (or not), to lie among others near death or already dead, to be dependent on and surrounded by wires and machines, intensive care imposes the most feared scenario: prolonged helplessness, often in pain. For years, hospital staff have known about "I.C.U. psychosis," the severe and not uncommon disorientation of patients reacting to the windowless, mechanical environment. For years, the only remedy has been to set a clock where the patient could see it.

The impact of the intensive care unit on the American way of dying has been profound, for it is there that contemporary medicine routinely eliminates the primary actor, the patient, from the ritual of dying. This is done by first selecting uncommonly passive patients in crisis. Medicine then perfected the way of artificially sustaining the clinically (if not legally) dead patient and replacing the old rituals of professional-patient interaction with emergency medical intervention, that is, professional team management of machines and bodies. Dying in this context is not something the individual patient, potentially a living corpse, really does, since it is a matter of the staff's withdrawing life supports. It has also become increasingly unclear what responsibility the once "masters of death" assume in hospital death scenarios. With few exceptions, modern physicians are revolted by death, leaving to nurses the "dirty work" of interacting with grieving families, the actual release of the patient from support machines, and ministering to the dead body.

Dying at Home

Recalling a time, long gone, when people died at home, Michel Foucault describes the family's gaze fixed on the sick person as full of "the vital force of benevolence and the discretion of hope." The contemporary alternative of dying at home guarantees no such comfort. Yet many households, prepared or not, must accept the prospect of such caretaking, even though the patient's death at the last minute takes place in the hospital.

Since the introduction of D.R.G.'s in 1983, the allowable length of hospital stay for Medicare patients has been sharply decreased. Growing numbers of chronically ill and elderly people are being cared for by relatives. But the family context has its problems: emotional ambivalence, instability, isolation from the larger community, and even violence. Hospice care, once hailed as the humane alternative to dying in the hospital, provides only minor support in terms of supplies and service. Family members, especially women, are left with the daily responsibility for patient care, which now often includes complex regimens of infusion drugs, intravenous feeding, oxygen support, and physical therapy. For most of the elderly, long-term nursing home care is economically not feasible. Hospitals have no room for those who are dying slowly—but then who does?

The toll of rejection may be seen in the increasing rate of suicide among the elderly. Between 1981 and 1986, suicides among people over sixty-five rose sharply, from 12.6 per 100,000 to 21.8. Starvation, refusal of medication, and guns were the principal means. How such private decisions are reached or even if they can be counted as rational, we do not know, although fear of being a burden is frequently reported in anecdotes. Such a fear itself is not irrational. Government and professional support for home care is minimal. Home-care providers receive scant training for the technical tasks they perform, no provision for relief, and no credit for the round-the-clock time they give. Having little or no reimbursement incentives, physicians generally ignore patients cared for at home. Cost coverage for home care varies with the insurance carrier. Even under private insurance plans, many items must be paid for out-of-pocket. In the last ten years, unregulated commercial agencies have taken over the growing, multi-billion dollar home-care industry and have inflated the retail cost of everything—needles, gauze, plastic tubing, rubber sheets, bed rentals, and drugs—in ways that parallel hospital charges for aspirin and the price of Pentagon coffee pots.

As death re-enters the American household, it is tamed only by the resources a family or perhaps only a single relative or friend can muster. Maybe the community has a free slot in the hospice program, maybe the physician will do more than telephone, maybe a member of the clergy will visit. But there are no guarantees. If the scenario of hospital death is daunting, so too is the vision of a drawn-out, painful expiration, resented and uncomforted by those intimates or the intimate to whom one is a burden. The choice to refuse medication or even food may be rational, if one truly believes it is time to die. But the rationale "I am only a burden" threatens all of us, for we are all at some time in our lives completely dependent on others.

Confronting Death

The present controversy surrounding physician-assisted suicide and rational suicide in general may be all to the good, if it promotes change in our institutions. How many people would be interested in a quick (six minutes), painless death in a parked van (the scenario for Janet Adkins, the first user of Kevorkian's mercitron machine), if hospitals and homes provided a more humane context for dying? Or is it that Americans, Puritans still, ask for nothing more than clean sheets and a morphine drip? This may be true. The rational suicides reported in the media all have a tidy, pain-free aura about them.

Critics, such as Mitford and Ariès, accurately identified our cultural denial of death as a serious aberration. We want death to never happen, to be a non-experience, or an event that cannot threaten our dignity. Yet, as the philosopher Paul Ramsey used to say, there is nothing at all dignified about dying—one might add, nor happy either. Death must be seen for what it is—cruelly inevitable, a painful rendering, our finitude—if we are to understand the human condition and even begin to ask about the meaning of life. Death is momentous, in the general and in the specific. For the dying person, spirit and body are inescapably involved in a final reckoning. No witness can be untouched, except by a distortion of the most fundamental truth, that we are mortal. The distance between us and the dying person is only an accident of time.

It is this sense of mortality we try to hide from and the reason we have created institutions of denial. Oddly enough, we even deny the extent to which these institutions contribute to our problems. In the innumerable debates and discussions about death, the focus remains on individual strategies, as if, for example, one person's choice of suicide over protracted terminal illness constituted a justification in itself, prompted by psychology, legitimated by one's will, and with no social consequences or meaning. Yet our hospitals are strange and alienating environments to the extent that they obfuscate this truth of mortality by therapeutic experimentalism, intensive care, and also the "harvesting" of organs from living corpses. Our homes are threatening to the extent that people are left in isolation to deal with life as a burden and death as an obscenity. The quick-fix suicide machine or the plastic bag method described in *Final Exit* might relieve the individual of woe and suffering, but what about the rest of us, who will dutifully attend to our living wills and then await the worst? We know that death is not obscene; it cannot by itself deprave us. But it is frightening in its familiarity and cannot be simply planned away. Rather, we should envision institutional reforms.

We need physicians educated to say more to the dying patient than "Have a nice trip" (Kevorkian's farewell to Janet Adkins). We need hospitals with staff motivated to give humane attention, not overtreatment, to the dying. We need compensation for families that give home care so that they can afford to be kind and old people can die in relative peace. Death is indeed a wild beast of sorts. These are ways to tame it.

READINGS SUGGESTED BY THE AUTHOR

Philippe Ariès. *Western Attitudes Toward Death*. Baltimore, Md.: Johns Hopkins University Press, 1974.

Susan DiGiacomo. "Biomedicine in the Cultural System: An Anthropologist in the Kingdom of the Sick," in *Encounters with Biomedicine: Case Studies in Medical Anthropology,* Hans Baer (ed.). New York: Gordon and Breach Science Publishers, 1987.

Susan Sontag. *Illness as Metaphor*. New York: Farrar, Straus, and Giroux, 1988.

COMING SOON:
YOUR NEIGHBORHOOD T.S.C.[3]

Retired pathologist Jack Kevorkian, also known as "Dr. Death," pleads his case to legalize doctor-assisted suicide in front of a Sunday congregation at St. Paul's Presbyterian Church in Livonia, Michigan. He is kicking off a ballot drive for a state constitutional amendment to secure this "right." The packed audience includes friends and relatives of most of the 20 people he has helped commit suicide since 1990, as well as the state executive director of the Hemlock Society, dedicated to suicide rights. The host pastor is an avid supporter. Dr. Kevorkian implacably asserts what he sees as the bottom line: "the right not to have to suffer." "This is really a right that already exists, and one we already have, but which we have to put in writing because of human irrationality. Every reasonable adult is going to have to realize that if he votes 'no' on this, he is throwing his right away."

[3]Article by Peter J. Bernardi, S. J., doctoral candidate in systematic theology at The Catholic University of America. This article originally appeared in *America* 170:6–9 Ap 30 '94, and has been expanded by the author for this compilation. Copyright © 1994 by Peter J. Bernardi. Reprinted with permission.

Kevorkian's simple logic resembles the glare of a single un-shaded light bulb hanging in a bare cell. The cell contains a solitary inmate in pain who wants to end it all. Once again, the complex texture of human life has been deceptively and insidiously reduced to the unthinking slogan, "right to choose." Using this logic, he has tied the Michigan legal system in knots and convinced jurors that administering carbon monoxide is mere pain relief.

Where have we heard this "reasoning" before? Derek Humphry, founder of the Hemlock Society which promotes "suicide rights," was asked in an interview why the euthanasia movement had picked up momentum in recent years. (Since 1990, two referenda that would have legalized euthanasia were defeated in California and the state of Washington by rather slim margins. Efforts to legalize physician-assisted suicide have been stymied for the moment in several other states.)

He responded that Roe v. Wade was the turning point. Even Humphry, the high priest of suicide, notes the connection between the legal victory of abortion rights and the growing demand for suicide rights. For when the "right to choose" to kill unborn babies was enshrined in law, founded on the "right to privacy," the suicide rights movement got new energy and legitimacy. A database search has turned up at least 34 termination-of-treatment cases that cite Roe v. Wade. The Circuit Court of Michigan in Michigan v. Kevorkian ruled that Michigan's statutory ban on assisted suicide was unconstitutionally overbroad because it interfered with the right to commit a "rational" suicide. The court relies heavily on Roe—which means there is a "slippery slope" leading from abortion rights to suicide rights. In May, 1994, Federal Judge Barbara Rothstein explicitly used Roe when she struck down the State of Washington's law banning assisted suicide as an unwarranted restriction on the right to privacy. These judicial decisions are on appeal and undoubtedly the Supreme Court will be asked to adjudicate the matter.

"Slippery slope" is a moral argument used to oppose a proposed action on the grounds that a principle is being conceded that has pernicious extensions and applications, perhaps not even envisaged by its original proponents. Ideas and practices have logical consequences. The experience of legalized abortion offers an obvious and striking case study of a slippery slope. Once the privacy principle was so legally enshrined in Roe as to allow the taking of innocent human life, it has become increasingly difficult, if not impossible, to brake the descent. A momentum has been established whereby the former presumption in favor of human life has given way to myriad forms of rationalizing and excusing the taking of life. Who would have dreamt in 1973 that by 1993 abortions would increase to 1.6 million annually? Very few of these abortions have to do with the "hard" cases of pregnancy as a result of rape or incest or of threat to the mother's life. Most abortions are now motivated by lifestyle reasons.

The suicide rights lobby is trying to push us farther down the slope. Once again the "hard" cases are trumpeted to attract sympathy and the "right to choose" rhetoric is invoked as reason for legalization. Huge numbers of abortions have resulted from the Roe decision, and it can hardly be alarmist to envision similar consequences if assisted suicide is legalized. Just as most abortions now are no longer "hard case" but "convenience" abortions, so will the circle of candidates for assisted suicide inevitably widen.

Indeed, Jack Kevorkian has given candid and chilling indications of his desire to extend "suicide rights." In an address to the National Press Club in Washington, D.C., on October 27, 1992, he asserted that "every disease that shortens life no matter how much is terminal." Who, then, are his potential "clients?" According to him, terminal cancer patients with but 6 months to live comprise only 10% of the people who "need" assisted suicide. This larger needy group, in his estimation, includes quadriplegics, people with M.S. and sufferers from severe arthritis!

A realistic assessment of our society suggests a multiplicity of cultural factors that will only accelerate the slide down this slippery slope. For one, there is widespread violence that blunts our sensitivity to the value of human life. Whether it is General Colin Powell's remark during the Persian Gulf War that the Iraqi soldiers would be crushed like roaches or the fact of 1.6 million unborn babies being butchered in the abortion mills, the same message is propagated: human life can be objectified and snuffed out if killing offers an advantage to the national or individual interest. When it is an encumbrance, there is little or no presumption in favor of human life.

Then there is our societal lack of patience. Change the technology—for example, increasingly speedy computers—and we "raise" our expectations. Waiting a few extra milliseconds becomes a burden. It is not a social climate that encourages the patient bearing of ills.

The fragmentation of the family and the scattering of the

extended family contribute to the epidemic of lifeless loneliness. For too many people, human relationships that once might have reminded them that they are worth more than their social utility have eroded. Assisted suicide offers an attractive "solution" for avoiding the burdens and loneliness of old age. Suicide studies indicate that single, elderly white men have proportionately the highest rate of suicide. In contrast, elderly black women have the lowest rate. Is religious faith a factor here?

And we are a society that prizes being in control, being in the driver's seat. Is not doctor-assisted suicide the ultimate if illusory control whereby one is master of one's destiny? Then death and the dying process are viewed mechanically: something to master, not a mysterious reality to submit to.

But the hidden foundation under the moral platform of the suicide-rights activists is the unexamined attitude that suffering is a complete evil. As a society we find any sort of suffering increasingly difficult to bear. But the greatest works of literature, like Sophocles's "Oedipus Rex" and Shakespeare's "King Lear" teach us that suffering affords the possibility of unimagined human growth, that growth in love and wisdom are potential fruits of suffering. Who has not been inspired and enriched by real-life stories of people courageously and patiently bearing pain and suffering, faithful to a destiny that eludes our capacity to fully fathom?

The film "Shadowlands" offers an example of the humanizing impact of heroism in the face of suffering and inevitable death. The story is based on the true-life love relationship between the Oxford don, C. S. Lewis, and an American woman named Joy Gresham. They come to share a depth of love that only the opacity of suffering and death, courageously faced without trying to control the outcome, could bring about. There is even an intense beauty to the dying process for those who have eyes to see. Philip Land, S. J., remarked not long before his death at age 82: "Have you noticed how much beauty goes into dying?"

On the other hand, it is not surprising to learn that, when Dr. Kevorkian was asked in a newspaper interview in the *Oakland Press* (Oakland County, Michigan, is where he has "staged" his assisted suicides) what he thought happened after death, he responded tersely: "You rot."

Are there any moral footholds to brake our descent? With the "right to privacy" legally enshrined by Roe and the cost containment mentality that has come to dominate health care in our society, there is not going to be much help coming from the legal and medical business fields. The various faith traditions must use their moral force to brake this descent. For example, Catholic moral teaching makes the crucial distinction that forbids the direct taking of life (euthanasia) but allows the withholding of extraordinary means to maintain life so that nature may take its course. Kevorkian rejected this distinction as well as the Hippocratic Oath in the *Oakland Press* interview. He predicted that some religious groups will "spare no expense" to defeat his Michigan "mercy" amendment. Fortunately, Kevorkian's efforts to stigmatize opposition to assisted suicide as religious zealotry failed to mobilize sufficient voter support for his ballot initiative. For the moment, the efforts to legalize euthanasia in Michigan have been blocked.

Ultimately, the religious conviction that life is a gift from God which we are not free to end on our terms is the most effective motive for remaining opposed to doctor-assisted self-killing. But what effect would that argument have on someone who is not religious or who does not believe in God?

It is possible, in fact, to argue against assisted suicide without using religious arguments. Reflective people not moved by faith ought to consider the "slippery slope" experience of abortion before they assent to Kevorkian's logic. The words Edmund Burke wrote in 1790 deserve their reflection: "The effect of liberty to individuals is, that they may do what they please: We ought to see what it will please them to do, before we risk congratulations, which may be soon turned into complaints."

If assisted suicide is legalized, then, in the not too distant future, clinics are going to open up in rather nondescript "professional" services buildings. Perhaps they will be adjacent to abortion clinics. In front of these clinics, orange-vested escorts with sympathetic faces will protectively shepherd their clients to the front door, keeping them at arm's length from those "anti-choice fanatics" who would question their "right to choose." That is, suicide on demand, available in a clinically professional atmosphere where staff in reassuring white uniforms are dedicated to your "choice not to suffer." One thing is certain: These staff persons won't have to deal with unsatisfied customers suffering from post-suicide trauma.

There will be the media campaign aided by linguistic censors to insure that religious "zealots" do not impose their moral categories. Euphemisms will be coined to eviscerate the moral content of assisted-suicide. Humphry's euphemism "final exit" will not catch on. It conjures up the diabolic "final solution." How about "termination-of-suffering" clinics, T.S.C.'s for short?

The suicide rights lobby will keep the spotlight on liberation from unbearable suffering and on the right to choose. The secular media, claiming dedication to free speech, will suppress accurate information about the astounding breakthroughs in pain management, and will largely ignore programs like Hospice that offer support for the terminally ill and their families.

The T.S.C.'s will network with nursing homes and organ-donor businesses. Indeed, Kevorkian favors an "auction" for the buying and selling of human organs. He considers the donation of organs one of the "positives" of assisted suicide.

Our society is indeed on a slippery slope. The slide down this slope could turn into a plunge over a precipice. The "right to privacy" is law and the "right to choose" is the slogan of the era. Morality has been made captive to such legality, and Dr. Kevorkian has a wide and sympathetic following. The culture of death bids fair to extend its domain.

(Author's note: On November 8, 1994, state of Oregon voters narrowly approved the first doctor assisted-suicide measure in our nation's history. Oregon has become the first jurisdiction in the world to legalize such a measure. The venerable Hippocratic Oath by which doctors promise not to give "deadly medicine to anyone if asked, nor suggest any such counsel" is now under direct legal attack.)

THE SUICIDE MACHINE[4]

The mercitron, Jack Kevorkian's suicide machine, was invented in 1989 and displayed on television on the *Donahue Show*. The mercitron delivers, on demand, (the patient pushes a plunger) a lethal dosage of sodium penthothal and potassium into the veins of the individual hooked up to its valves. On June 4, 1990,

[4]Article by Norman K. Denzin, professor of sociology at the University of Illinois, Urbana-Champagne. From *Society* 29:7–10 Jl/Ag '92. Copyright © 1992 by *Society*. Reprinted with permission.

Kevorkian announced in the *New York Times* that he helped a woman, Janet Adkin, commit suicide. She had seen his machine work on the *Donahue Show*. Here is how he described her death in *Free Inquiry:*

I started the intravenous dripper, which released a salt solution through a needle into her vein, and I kept her arm tied down so she wouldn't jerk it. This was difficult as her veins were fragile. And then once she decided she was ready to go, she just hit the switch and the device cut off the saline drip and through the same needle released a solution of thiopental that put her to sleep in ten to fifteen seconds. A minute later, through the same needle flowed a lethal solution of potassium chloride.

This is how assisted suicide with the mercitron works. Cool, mechanical death, a reversal of medical technology, for, as Jean Baudrillard has put it, the "increasing cerebral capacities of machines would normally lead to a technological purification of the body." Kevorkian's death machine reverses the code of life. Now medicine kills.

In a swift push of the plunger, in an ecstasy of metastasis, my body moves from one cancerous form to another. My body, coupled to a machine, undergoes a metamorphosis. Eros and Thanatos collide on the doctor's table; an ecstasy of seduction. The end of my body and my history. The fatal moment. Euphoria. I have beaten the death culture. My life is in my hands. A machine is doing this for me. I am killing myself! And I have a smile on my face. Or do I? When I die will I still be hooked to this machine?

Kevorkian calls this planned death, a rational system that honors self-determination. He distinguishes this form of dying from medicide or euthanasia, which are deaths performed by a medical professional. To date at least six chronically ill individuals have died with the help of Kevorkian's machine: forty-three-year-old Sherry Miller, fifty-eight-year-old Marjorie Wantz, fifty-four-year-old Janet Adkins (who had Alzheimer's disease), two women from Oakland, California, and Gary Sloan, a forty-four-year-old terminally ill dentist, who was advised (they exchanged letters) by Kevorkian on how to kill himself with a suicide machine. On February 5, 1991, an Oakland county judge ordered Kevorkian to stop using his suicide machines. In the same week he faced a preliminary hearing in Oakland county on two counts of murder. On February 18, 1992, the *New York Times* reported that Kevorkian was to be tried for murder in the State of Michigan in the assisted deaths of Sherry Miller and Marjorie Wantz. An earlier murder charge against the doctor (for the assisted death of Janet Adkins) had been dropped since Michigan does not have a law against assisted-suicide deaths.

A Death Culture

The mercitron is the postmodern method of death. Suited for those who have the luxury and the time to seek a kinder form of death, the mercitron is for the middle classes. It is not an option for the walking and wounded members of America's ethnic underclasses, among whom violent deaths are everyday occurrences, and drug addiction and alcoholism are the preferred softer, gentler forms of suicide and self-annihilation. The suicide machine must be located in its historical period. America is a death culture. Americans are preoccupied with extending life and preventing death. Hospitals and physicians are the gatekeepers to life and death. Death is seen as reversing the codes that organize everyday life (life-death, masculine-feminine, subject-object). In a single stroke death annihilates that which has denied its existence, life.

And so in dying one embraces finiteness. People turn their back on science, rationality, medicine, and maybe religion. By attempting to control, prolong, and manage life rationally and scientifically, our society reveals its deep commitment to a liberal, Enlightenment philosophy that has lost touch with the contemporary moment. Kevorkian is not alone in his desire to bring a different form of death and dying into American culture.

In mid-1991 Derek Humphry's book *Final Exit: The Practicalities of Self-Deliverance and Assisted Suicide for the Dying* went to the top of the bestseller lists with sales of over 500,000 for the year. In 1991 membership in the Hemlock Society, a group dedicated to the rights of the terminally ill to choose voluntary euthanasia, climbed to over 38,000 with seventy chapters. By 1992 euthanasia societies in the Netherlands, Britain, France, and the United States were lobbying for legal reforms permitting euthanasia. On December 1, 1991, the Patient Self-Determination Act became law in the United States. Enacted a few short years after the right-to-die celebrity cases involving Nancy Cruzan, Karen Ann Quinlan, and Roswell Gilbert, this law mandates that all health-care providers receiving Medicare or Medicaid inform patients over the age of eighteen of their right to plan in advance for their care. The living will has become commonplace in America, and hospitals are now routinely asking patients if they wish to make a death plan.

Right-to-die groups, influenced by the Hemlock Society, have started to appear in other states besides California, including Oregon and Washington, and New York where the choice-in-dying group promotes patients' rights to refuse care. All states, except Nebraska and Pennsylvania, now have laws that honor at least one form of the living will. On average 5,800 Americans die each day. Over 75 percent of these deaths are timed or negotiated.

Middle Class Americans are taking death seriously. The cultural taboos of suicide for reasons of health have been broken. Suicide now ranks as the eighth leading cause of death in the United States (heart diseases are number one). By the year 2000, the largest age group in the United States will be the sixty-five and over category and suicide by the elderly will continue to be a leading cause of death for this group, as it will also be for the chronically ill, including those dying from AIDS. Active and passive euthanasia will be taken for granted as the dying members of this culture seek their private forms of death. (Humphry's book is a shopper's guide in this respect, listing among methods of death, electrocution, hanging, drowning, shooting, asphyxiation from car exhausts or ovens, ingesting poisonous plants or cyanide, freezing, self-starvation, and lethal dosages of various drugs including codine, diazepan, butabarbital, and pentobarbital.)

Medicide, assisted suicides, planned deaths, hospice-managed deaths, and the new medical humanism, are now everywhere present in our culture. Nowadays, to paraphrase C. Wright Mills, Americans are taking death into their own hands. A self-managed death is the only real symbolic violence they can wage against the impersonal, structural violence of the postmodern moment. Only in death, claim the members of the Hemlock, medicide, right-to-die, and choice-in-dying movements, can one escape the panoptic eye of an inhumane medical establishment. This establishment and its technologies have turned what goes on inside the human body into a new regime of signs and symbols that no longer have any reference to life itself.

The postmodern moment is characterized, as Max Weber and C. Wright Mills predicted, by the irrational rationalization and bureaucratization of everyday life. Large technological structures, including the medical establishment and the health care industries, exert ever greater control over the human body and its destiny. Throughout this century the medical establishment has wielded power over life and death. This system of control, Arthur Frank observes, has led to the progressive medicalization of everyday life. Today more and more issues, including who can work when and where, are decided by medical opinion. Health, life, and death have become commodities only few can afford, and health-care rationing (who lives and who dies) is now largely a matter of wealth and status.

An increasingly hospital-based medicine has eroded the traditional doctor-patient model of treatment, while clinical judgment has become a matter of laboratory technologies. As Arthur Frank has noted: "My body is decentered in videotapes of angiograms and ultrasounds, in files of CAT scan images, in graphs of blood cell counts, and serum levels. When I am asked how I feel, it is these to which I refer and which refer to me. In the medical simulacrum I lose myself in my image . . . the reality of how I feel passes into signs without feeling."

This regime of power and control is now under attack. Those drawn to the new forms of self-determined death are no longer willing to accept the medical establishment's place in this life and death equation. The growing attraction of the assisted-suicide movement reflects the belief that doctors and hospitals have gone too far in their care of the terminally ill. Life at any cost is no longer desirable, especially when the last days of life in an intensive-care unit can cost $100,000 or more. People are seeking a cheaper way to die, while coming to the conclusion that they are no longer willing to prolong the dying process needlessly. They seek other systems of signs and meanings that will give them the illusion of control over their lives. This is where Kevorkian's mercitron again enters the picture.

The Ideology Behind the Machine

Kevorkian's arguments rest on a new medical humanism that would allow patient and family to determine the moment of death. This he calls a "positive" death. According to Kevorkian, this humanism carries three benefits: a reduction in patient suffering, less psychological pain for family and friends, and a savings in resources that would be spent on prolonged care. The benefits, he argues, do not counterbalance the loss of human life. Hence, he adds one more benefit, of major importance: the ability of the patient who opts for a planned death to save the life of another. Under Kevorkian's system the dying patient is asked how his or her body should be used to save the life of another human being. A patient might, he suggests, decide to donate vital organs, or undergo a critical medical experiment. So in dying the person contributes to science, medicine, society, and the lives of others.

The key to Kevorkian's model lies in the body's uses after death. He thus distinguishes between positive and negative death; negative death being defined as death without positive social, medical, or scientific consequence for society. Medicide produces positive death. All other forms of death our culture sanctions, including obligatory (death row), assisted (euthanasia), and optional suicide (mentally illness) produce negative death, a loss without meaning. His is an attempt to turn death into something positive, into both a merciful experience and a process that yields something "of real value to suffering humanity left behind."

Suicide Centers

From this reasoning derives the mercitron. This machine will be located in suicide centers. In these centers, centralized, rationally organized, well controlled, merciful, dignified deaths will occur. Ethical and experimental manipulations on the body will also be conducted. Because suicide and euthanasia carry negative connotations, Kevorkian offers the word *obitorium* (from the Latin *obitus,* meaning to go to meet death) for the center, and *obitiatry* (from *iatros* meaning doctor in Greek) for the speciality. Thus is born a new medical practitioner, the *obitiatrist,* a new medical speciality, *obitiatry,* "the doctoring of death to achieve some sort of beneficial result," as Kevorkian puts it. Obitiatry is positive medicide.

Obitoria would be staffed by experts who know how to use the mercitron. These medical specialists will consult with other specialists when the time comes to connect an individual to the mercitron. Every community will have a five-member group of obitiatry specialists who will vote on a given instance of medicide. All members of the group must agree before a death can occur. As these decisions are being made, dying individuals will fill out questionnaires concerning their decision to die. Everybody is thereby protected, as this final decision, which is a medical problem, is implemented. It can then be said that the patient died in order to save the lives of others.

Rational death. Science fiction now. Come to the *obitorium* to die. This is altruistic death with a vengeance. It asserts the primacy of the social over the individual, making a distinction between selfish (non-giving) and giving (the good) death. It reduces the existential phenomenon of patient suffering and the psychological pain and guilt for family and friends to minor benefits. These existential realities of death are erased in a single stroke, replaced by a new logic of the social and the scientific. This new logic subordinates the body, its history, and its parts to a higher goal: service to humankind and the perpetuation of human life.

Under Kevorkian's model the opposition between the exchange, use and symbolic value of the body is erased. Traditionally, medicine has assumed that a given system of exchange would allow a particular commodity, health care, to be purchased and used in the name of another commodity, good health, or a longer life. Use value was not implicated in the logic peculiar to exchange value, as Baudrillard points out. Any system would work. Any care giver would deliver care to any needy recipient. This model no longer exists. Kevorkian's model, like the one he opposes, commodifies the body in terms of its organs, which are donated at the moment of death, and turns the body into another exchange object. There is no longer any distinction between use and exchange value. There is no code that connects the two systems, no symbolic referent that would bring a body and its parts back to the life that donated the part. The signs of the body, as well as of life, have now become death and its residues, the parts no longer needed, will now be given to science and humanity.

Fatal Visions

The era of subversion and transgression has passed, the simulacrum (the truth which says there is no truth) has won. Life, death, love, sex, the stuff of life, have surpassed their own definitions. They have become, as Baudrillard argues, more "social than the social (the masses), fatter than the fat (obesity), more violent than the violent (terror), more sexual than sex (pornography), more real than the real (simulation), more beautiful than the beautiful (fashion). Hence, more beautiful than me you die, truer than me you die, more real than me you simulate, and more simulated than me you die." Death, the final symbolic act against the medical establishment, against society, against self and other, has now been transformed. One machine has replaced another. I simulate my death, you simulate your death. We produce video copies for our friends and loved ones, for all that is missing from the mercitron is a camera recording my death. You can watch me in those last seconds of my life, as the poisonous drug drips into my veins.

Baudrillard is wrong when he claims that "perhaps only death, the reversibility of death, is of a higher code than the code . . . this is the only symbolic violence worthy of the structural violence of the code." Even in death we cannot escape the code, for the new medicide movement requires that our bodies serve the higher goal of life itself.

Thus, in the desire to escape an older medical ethic and an Enlightenment set of social ideals, the new medical humanism advocated by Kevorkian ends by embracing what it started out to reject. And it does this with a vengeance. For if, when I die, I must consider what my life means to others, then I have not escaped the social net that had previously prolonged life for me and my fellows. Now I die early for another set of individuals. Who wins?

No longer can we just go gently into that good night. Even if, as the philosopher Martin Heidegger reminds us, we are born dying, our dying now becomes a matter of social planning, social concern, and commitments to higher ideals. Here at the end science fiction meets and even anticipates reality. Death machines, clean, antiseptically sterile obitoria, the new funeral homes, soft organ music playing, obitiatrists in white jackets, rows upon rows of mercitrons plugged into inert bodies, happy family members mingle in joy as their loved ones drift off into death, and behind closed doors their bodies are taken apart to be experimented upon.

Postmodern death has won. The social may be dead, but death is still alive and working well in the new obitoria. Here at the end we embrace a new kind of death. Cynicism is required. Not because more merciful forms of dying do not need to be imagined—they do. Rather it should be possible to imagine a form of dying that does not require the invention of new machines and new medical specialities. After all it was science, medicine and the new technologies that got us into this mess in the first place. Can we not imagine a new set of ethics that would allow individuals to determine their moment of death without all of the complications that accompany Kevorkian's suicide machine?

BIBLIOGRAPHY

An asterisk (*) preceding a reference indicates that the material or part of it has been reprinted in this book.

BOOKS AND PAMPHLETS

Aarons, Leroy. Prayers for Bobby: a mother's coming to terms with the suicide of her gay son. HarperSanFrancisco. '95.

Alvarez, A. The savage god: a study of suicide. Norton. '90.

Anthony, T. Mitchell. Suicide: knowing when your teen is at risk. Regal. '91.

Baker, James F. I don't want to live anymore: thoughts on suicide and its prevention. CES. '92.

Barnett, Terry J. Living wills and more. Everything you need to ensure that all your medical wishes are followed. Wiley. '93.

Battin, M. Pabst. The least worst death: essays in bioethics on the end of life. Oxford University Press. '94.

————. Ethical issues in suicide. Prentice-Hall. '94.

Beisser, Arnold R. A graceful passage: notes on the freedom to live or to die. Doubleday. '90.

Bergman, David B. Kids on the brink: understanding the teen suicide epidemic. PIA. '90.

Berman, Alan L., ed. Suicide prevention: case consultations. Springer. '90.

————— & Jobes, David A. Adolescent suicide: assessment and intervention. American Psychological Association. '91.

Betzold, Michael. Appointment with Doctor Death. Momentum. '93.

Blumenthal, Susan & Kupfer, David, eds. Suicide over the life cycle. American Psychological Association. '90.

Bongar, Bruce. The suicidal patient. American Psychological Association. '91.

Brill, Alida. Nobody's business: paradoxes of privacy. Addison-Wesley. '90.

Burnell, George M. Final choices. Insight. '93.

Cantor, Norman L. Advance directives and the pursuit of death with dignity. Indiana University Press. '93.

Carr, G. Lloyd & Carr, Gwendolyn C. The fierce goodbye: hope in the wake of suicide. InterVarsity. '90.

Chance, Sue. Stronger than death. Norton. '92.

Clemens, James T. Perspectives on suicide. Westminster John Knox. '90.

Cole, Harry & Jablow, Martha. One in a million. Little, Brown. '90.

Colen, B. D. The essential guide to a living will: how to protect your right to refuse medical treatment. Prentice Hall. '91.

Collins, Evan & Weber, Doron. The complete guide to living wills. Bantam. '91.

Colt, George Howe. The enigma of suicide. Summit. '91.

Conroy, David L. Out of the nightmare: recovery from depression and suicidal pain. New Liberty. '91.

Cook, John. How to help someone who is depressed or suicidal. Rubicon. '94.

Cosculluela, Victor. The ethics of suicide. Garland. '95.

Cox, Donald W. The struggle for death with dignity. Prometheus. '93.

Cox, Gerry R. & Fundis, Ronald J., eds. Spiritual, ethical, and pastoral aspects of death and bereavement. Baywood. '92.

Cundiff, David. Euthanasia is not the answer: a hospice physician's view. Humana. '92.

Davis, John M. & Sandoval, Jonathan. Suicidal youth: school-based intervention and prevention. Jossey-Bass. '91.

DeLeo, Laura. Suicide. Chelsea. '92.

Dworkin, R. M. Life's dominion: an argument about abortion, euthanasia, and individual freedom. Knopf. '93.

Elliott, Harold & Bailey, Brad. Suicide is not painless. WRS Group. '93.

Feldman, Fred. Confrontations with the reaper: a philosophical study of the nature and value of death. Oxford University Press. '92.

Flanders, Stephen. Suicide. Facts on File. '91.

Gardner, Sandra & Rosenberg, Gary. Teenage suicide. Messner. '90.

Gay, Kathlyn. The right to die. Milbrook. '93.

Glick, Henry R. The right to die. Columbia University Press. '92.

Green, Gerard. Coping with suicide: a pastoral aid. Columbia Press. '92.

Jacobs, Douglas, ed. Suicide and clinical practice. American Psychiatric Press. '92.

Jussim, Daniel. Euthanasia: the "right to die" issue. Enslow. '93.

Hammer, Signe. By her own hand: memoirs of a suicide's daughter. Soho. '91.

Harness-Overley, Patricia. A message of hope: for surviving the tragedy of suicide. Bradley. '92.

Hicks, Barbara B. Youth suicide: a comprehensive manual for prevention and intervention. National Educational Service. '90.

Hopkins, Sidney Jack. Suicide and its psychological influences: index of authors & subjects with guide for rapid research. ABBE. '94.

Humphry, Derek. Dying with dignity. Carol. '92.

———. Let me die before I wake. Hemlock Society. '91.

————. Final exit: the practicalities of self-deliverance and assisted suicide for the dying. Hemlock Society. '91.

———— & Wickett, Ann. The right to die. Hemlock Society. '90.

Hyde, Margaret O. & Forsyth, Elizabeth H. Suicide. Watts. '91.

Kevorkian, Jack. Prescription—medicide: the goodness of a planned death. Prometheus. '91.

Kirk, William G. Adolescent suicide. Research. '93.

Johnston, Brian. Death as a salesman: what's wrong with assisted suicide. New Regency. '94.

Landau, Elaine. The right to die. Watts. '93.

Lee, Robert G. & Morgan, Derek. Death rites: law and ethics at the end of life. Routledge. '94.

Leenaars, Antoon, ed. Life span perspectives on suicide. Plenum. '91.

————, et al., eds. Suicide and the older adult. Guildford. '92.

Lester, David, ed. Current concepts of suicide. Charles. '90.

————. Understanding and preventing suicide: new perspectives. Thomas. '90.

————. Understanding suicide: a case study approach. Nova Science. '93.

———— & Danto, Bruce L. Suicide behind bars: prediction and prevention. Charles Press. '93.

Logue, Barbara. Last rights: death control and the elderly in America. Lexington. '93.

Malcolm, Andrew H. Someday. Knopf. '91.

Market, Rita. Deadly compassion: the death of Ann Humphry and the truth about euthanasia. Morrow. '93.

Molloy, William. Vital choices. Viking. '93.

Moreland, James & Geisler, Norman. The life and death debate. Praeger. '90.

Neeley, G. Steven. The constitutional right to suicide: a legal and philosophical examination. Lang. '94.

Overberg, Kenneth R., ed. Mercy or murder? Euthanasia morality and public policy. Sheed & Ward. '93.

Patros, Philip G. & Shamoo, Tonia K. I want to kill myself: helping your child cope with depression and suicidal thoughts. Lexington. '93.

Peluso, Samuel L. To live and die with dignity: a guide to living wills. Vista. '91.

Prado, C. G. The last choice: preemptive suicide in advanced age. Greenwood. '90.

Rosenblatt, Stanley M. Murder or mercy: euthanasia on trial. Prometheus. '92.

Styron, William. Darkness visible. Random House. '90.

Tada, Joni. When is it right to die? Harper. '92.

Urofsky, Melvin. Letting go: death, dying, and the law. University of Oklahoma Press. '94.

Vaux, Kenneth L. Death ethics: religious and cultural values in prolonging and ending life. Trinity. '92.

Watts, Tim J. Last rites or last rights II: an updated, selective bibliography, 1986–1991. Vance bibliographies. '91.

Wertheimer, Alison. A special scar: the experiences of people bereaved by suicide. Routledge. '91.

Whitaker, Leighton & Slimak, Richard, eds. College student suicide. Haworth. '90.

Williams, Kate. A parent's guide for suicidal and depressed teens. Hazelden. '95.

Wrobleski, Adina. Suicide, survivors: a guide for those left behind. A. Wrobleski. '94.

ADDITIONAL PERIODICAL ARTICLES WITH ABSTRACTS

For those who wish to read more widely on the subject of suicide, this section contains abstracts of additional articles that bear on the topic. Readers who require a comprehensive list of materials are advised to consult the *Reader's Guide to Periodical Literature* and other Wilson indexes.

The law and assisted suicide. Robert F. Drinan. *America* 170:6–7 Je 4–11 '94

On May 3, 1994, Seattle, Washington, Federal Judge Barbara Rothstein issued the first judicial decision in U.S. history allowing physicians to hasten the death of a terminally ill patient who voluntarily and clearly asks a doctor to end his or her life. In her ruling, Rothstein noted that the suffering of a terminally ill person is a constitutionally protected privacy matter. She argued that if the law permits sick people to refuse nourishment or reject medical devices aimed at prolonging life, they should also have the right to methods of hastening death. While Catholic tradition does permit the withholding of extraordinary life-prolonging measures, it is still not clear how this principle applies to situations in which a patient wants to speed the arrival of certain death. Catholics must continue to uphold the belief that only God has the right to determine when life should end.

Doctors and suicide. Mark L. Fuerst. *American Health* 12:25 Ap '93

According to psychiatrist Herbert Hendin, director of the American Suicide Foundation, victims of a fatal disease who ask their doctors to help them kill themselves may suffer from treatable clinical depression. Hendin says that the terminally ill patients who are most vulnerable to suicidal impulses are those in excruciating pain and those who have just learned of their illnesses. He asserts that once the depression is treated, most patients want to live. He thinks that doctors should focus on treating suicidal symptoms, relieving pain, and helping the dying come to terms with death.

Manic depression: not for artists only. *American Health* 12:42 D '93

Some 2 million to 3 million Americans suffer from the mood disorder known as manic depression, also called bipolar illness. Afflicting men and women in equal numbers, the disorder manifests itself as manic (high-energy) episodes, as depression, or as bouts between the 2 extremes. Some may experience manic and depressive symptoms simultaneously. The disease is known to run in families, but researchers are still working to find the responsible gene. Two-thirds of manic-depressives go untreated, which is cause for concern because, as Johns Hopkins psychologist Kay Redfield Jamison notes, the disease tends to worsen if ignored. Many manic-depressives develop substance abuse problems, and about 15 percent to 20 percent eventually commit suicide. With ongoing treatment, however, up to 80 percent of manic-depressives experience significant improvement.

The wrong way to go. David Neff. *Christianity Today* 35:15 O 28 '91

Washington State's Initiative 119, which, if passed, would offer legal protection to doctors who perform active euthanasia, should be rejected as bad law and bad morality. The law fails to set up any regulatory procedure to monitor the process by which patients request and doctors perform euthanasia, and it capitalizes on the prevailing and illusory myth of personal autonomy. Instead of trying to legalize euthanasia, society would do better to concentrate on developing its present health care resources.

Hemlock Society: built on a myth? *Christianity Today* 35:51 D 16 '91

The recent suicide of Hemlock Society cofounder Ann Wickett and statements that she made prior to her death have raised questions about the depth of the proeuthanasia organization's compassion. In 1980, Wickett and her husband, Derek Humphry, cofounded the Hemlock Society to promote legislation to legalize assisted suicide for the terminally ill. Nine years later, Wickett was diagnosed with breast cancer, and her marriage dissolved. In a 1990 interview, Wickett criticized Humphry and the Hemlock Society's board members for failing to offer her any support during her illness. Moreover, Wickett left suicide notes implicating Humphry in the death of his first wife during the 1970s. Humphry, who says that he helped his first wife commit suicide but denies the accusation that he killed her, asserts that Wickett suffered from "emotional illness."

The euthanasia follies. *Commonweal* 121:3–4 Je 3 '94

Two recent court decisions have come down in favor of physician-assisted suicide. On May 2, in a trial that was full of confusing technicalities, a Michigan jury acquitted Dr. Jack Kevorkian on charges of assisting the suicide of a 30-year-old man who suffered from a degenerative nerve disease. Less easily dismissed is the May 3 ruling by Federal Judge Barbara Rothstein in Seattle, Washington, which not only legalizes euthanasia but also makes it a constitutionally protected right. The judge, who claimed that the Supreme Court's reasoning in Planned Parenthood v. Casey is "almost prescriptive" in allowing a terminally ill person to have a doctor assist in suicide, found no constitutionally meaningful difference between allowing to die and direct killing. She did, however, allow the Washington State law on physician-assisted suicide to stand pending appeal. It is to be hoped that the Supreme Court will correct the judge's error.

Euthanasia in the 1990s: dying a "good" death. Rosemarie Tong. *Current* [Washington, D.C.] 354:27–33 Jl/Ag '93

An article excerpted from "The Possibility of Dying a 'Good' Death," which appeared in the March issue of The World & I. Widespread interest in euthanasia is not a sign of a death-driven culture but of one enamored with life and nearly obsessive about its well-being. Many people want assurance from their doctors that any pain and suffering they experience will be adequately relieved. For this reason, when faced with the possibility of a painful death or lingering in a severely incapacitated state, some are turning to euthanasia. So far the public, physicians, and the legal system have not reached a consensus as to how to approach euthanasia. The writer examines voluntary, nonvoluntary, and involuntary passive and active euthanasia; discusses the cases of Karen Quinlan, Nancy Cruzan, Helga Wanglie, and an Indiana "Baby Doe" with Down's syndrome and esophageal atresia who was allowed to die; and describes "aid-in-dying" as practiced by physicians.

Killing machines: doctors and suicide. George J. Annas. *Current* [Washington, D.C.] 337:17–20 N '91

An article reprinted from "Killing Machines," which appeared in the March/April 1991 Hastings Center Report. Ethicists concerned about physician Jack Kevorkian and the "suicide machine" that he used to help Janet Adkins die were perhaps more upset at the machine than at the act itself. In the military, chemical and biological weapons are seen as unfair and unethical tools that blur the distinction between warfare and murder. Such weapons are considered different in kind from conventional weapons, even though they are intended to do the same things. Just as soldiers are expected to adhere to the ethics and rules of warfare, physicians must obey the ethics and rules of medicine. In cases of suicide or assisted suicide, therefore, the means do matter. Kevorkian's machine is like other technologies in that it seems to remove accountability from the user. People may prefer to dwell on the ethics of the machine because technology, unlike death, seems clean and controllable.

Pulling a friend back from the brink of suicide. Susan Goodman. *Current Health 2* 17:18–19 F '91

Suicide is the second most common cause of death among teenagers. Experts know that suicidal behavior is often preceded by depression, which can be triggered by loneliness, family problems, pressure, and a host of other factors. Adolescence is a difficult time that is marked by the need to carve out individual values and a sexual identity. Today's teenagers also have to cope with drugs, the media's messages about violence, and the pressure to succeed in a society that values material success. Suicidal teenagers are often frozen in a moment of extreme sadness, anger, or guilt. They cannot imagine a time when they can bring their problem and feelings into perspective. Advice on how to help a friend who is suffering from depression is provided.

The at-risk students schools continue to ignore. Del Stover. *The Education Digest* 57:36–40 My '92

An article condensed from the March 1992 issue of the Executive Educator. AIDS has forced schools to tackle such controversial issues as condoms and sexual behavior, but homosexuality remains a sensitive topic. As a result, gay students are not receiving the attention that they deserve as a high risk group. Society's general antipathy toward gays has left gay youths frightened and uncertain about their self worth and very vulnerable to depression, drug use, school failure, and suicide. In 1989, the U.S. Department of Health and Human Services reported that 30 percent of all teens who commit suicide are gay and that gay teens are 2 to 3 times more likely than other teens to attempt suicide. Some gay youth are further endangered when they turn to sexual experimentation or seek adult companionship without considering the risks. Several ways that schools can help gay students and programs developed specifically for gay students are discussed.

Why is he still loose? Malcolm S. Forbes, Jr. *Forbes* 152:25–6 Ag 2 '93

The fact that Jack Kevorkian has not and probably will not be tried for murder, or at least manslaughter, says a lot about the confused state of

American mores. Americans seem to be more concerned with the "right to die" than with helping those who are struggling to live. Most people who attempt to take their lives, and many of those who succeed, are really crying out for help. Kevorkian-like killers use "death with dignity" to rationalize their actions, but those they assist are actually people who need reassurance from family, friends, and community that the real dignity is their not giving in to despair. Ironically, the growing popularity of suicide and euthanasia comes at a time when medicine has greatly reduced the amount of pain people must bear.

The West's deepening cultural crisis. Richard Eckersley. *The Futurist* 27:8–12 N/D '93

A cultural crisis in the West is wreaking havoc with the psychological well-being of people, especially teenagers and young adults. Among the indicators of the growing despair in the West are increasing drug use and crime rates, rampant violence, widespread depressive illness, and an alarming rise in the suicide rate. Some assert that these problems are caused by such things as unemployment, poverty, child abuse, and family breakdowns, but the real cause is the failure of Western culture to provide a sense of meaning, belonging, and purpose to people's lives as well as a framework of values in which to live. The article discusses the sources of cultural decay, how children view the future, and the manner in which science can be used to create a more harmonious society.

Should doctors be allowed to help terminally ill patients commit suicide? Derek Humphry. *Health* [San Francisco] 7:22 My/Je '93

The writer, who is the founder of the Hemlock Society and author of Final Exit, explains why he favors legalizing physician-assisted suicide for patients who are irreversibly, terminally, and hopelessly ill. He argues that decisions about the quality of life are the sole right of the individual. He also notes that people who are depressed or who feel that they are a burden to their families should be counseled and helped to live.

The legacy of Sue Rodriguez. *Maclean's* 107:22–8 F 28 '94

A special section focuses on the Canadian debate over assisted suicide. The death of Sue Rodriguez, an amyotrophic lateral sclerosis (ALS) sufferer who chose to end her own life with the help of a physician, has put a human face on the abstract moral discussion about assisted suicide. The assistance that Rodriguez received on Feb. 12 is illegal under Canadian law. The 43-year-old resident of Saanich, B.C., had asked the courts to overturn the existing law, but her request was denied. Many Canadians have expressed sympathy with Rodriguez's plight and agree that assisted suicides like hers should be legal, but some fear that easing the law may be a first step toward euthanasia without consent. Articles discuss the differing styles of 2 Canadian right-to-die advocacy groups and the career of

MP Svend Robinson, a New Democrat from British Columbia who is sponsoring right-to-die legislation in Canada's Parliament.

Opting out. Frank A. Oski. *The Nation* 258:77+ Ja 24 '94

For his advocacy and practice of active euthanasia, Jack Kevorkian should be regarded as a hero. Kevorkian developed an efficient suicide machine that enables terminally ill patients to take their own lives painlessly. He has endured first-degree murder charges, jail, and a hunger strike. The writer distinguishes passive euthanasia from active euthanasia, suggests guidelines for the use of active euthanasia, and discusses the history of the U.S. movement to legalize euthanasia, the legal status of assisted suicide in most states, and the views of physicians on the issue.

My obsession with life. Jack Lessenberry. *New Perspectives Quarterly* 11:35–7 Wint '94

Part of a special section on the changing boundaries of life and death. In an interview, Michigan doctor Jack Kevorkian, who has assisted 20 people in committing suicide, discusses the individual's right to end his or her life, the reasons why the medical profession opposes him, his counseling of patients who are ill and seeking death, the chances for euthanasia's one day becoming legal, his idea of auctioning off organs for transplant, and his suggestion that medical experiments and organ harvesting be performed on willing criminals who are condemned to death.

Live and let die. Richard John Neuhaus. *National Review* 46:40 Ap 4 '94

The "right to die" movement continues to expand. Most states have already enacted "living will" and "health-care proxy" laws, which specify what kinds of life support are to be withdrawn or withheld in the event of mental incompetency and allow patients to appoint other people to make decisions for them, respectively. Some laws even allow the withdrawal of nutrition from patients who are not "terminal" in the traditional sense. Right to die activists are now advocating "automatic proxy" statutes that would give designated people power to make life-and-death decisions for incompetent patients who never appointed a proxy or signed a living will. The activists are also pushing to deny life support even when patients or their families want such support. Having failed to win referendums in several states, proponents of euthanasia and physician-assisted suicide are now going to court.

Kevorkian vows to keep fighting laws barring assisted suicide. *New York Times* [Late New York Edition, Section 1] 43 D 18 '94 (Dec. 17)

Dr. Jack Kevorkian, a retired pathologist who has helped 21 severely ill people end their lives since 1990, has criticized the Michigan

Supreme Court for ruling that assisted suicide is a crime and has vowed to continue to crusade for what he calls "a fundamental human right." The court said that even without a law, suicide assistance "may be prosecuted as a common-law felony" that would carry a five-year prison term.

Vancouver AIDS suicides botched. Clyde H. Farnsworth. *New York Times* [Late New York Edition] C12 Je 14 '94

Canadian researcher Russel D. Ogden has completed a study of assisted suicide among people with AIDS. Ogden, whose study was submitted for a master's degree in criminal law at Simon Fraser University in Vancouver, discovered repeated examples of back-alley euthanasia among AIDS patients. He found that half of the 34 assisted suicide attempts he studied were bungled, increasing the patients' suffering instead of ending it.

Panel tells Albany to resist legalizing assisted suicide. Elisabeth Rosenthal. *New York Times* [Late New York Edition] A1+ My 26 '94

The New York State Task Force on Life and the Law released a report yesterday in which it recommended unanimously that the state resist pressure to legalize physician-assisted suicide for the terminally ill. The report comes amid growing support for the practice, as voiced in polls, state legislatures, and courts around the U.S.

Right-to-die group stages a rally for Kevorkian. *New York Times* [Late New York Edition, Section 1] 36 S 19 '93

About 100 members of a group called Friends of Dr. Kevorkian rallied in support of Jack Kevorkian, a retired pathologist who assists the suicides of the terminally ill, outside his apartment in a Detroit suburb on Sept. 18. After he publicly detailed his role in the suicide in August of a man with Lou Gehrig's disease, Kevorkian was ordered to stand trial under Michigan's new law making assisted suicide punishable by up to 4 years in prison.

Kevorkian aids in suicide, no. 17, near police station. Don Terry. *New York Times* [Late New York Edition] A14 Ag 5 '93

On August 4, Dr. Jack Kevorkian helped Thomas W. Hyde, Jr., a 30-year-old man who was suffering from amyotrophic lateral sclerosis, or Lou Gehrig's disease, to commit suicide in a van parked near a city police station in Belle Isle, Michigan. At a news conference, Kevorkian dared authorities to prosecute him under Michigan's new but contested law that makes it a felony to assist in a suicide. Passage of the law was spurred by a widespread distress over the growing number of suicides assisted by Kevorkian.

Suicide doctor is jailed in Detroit amid a threat to starve himself. *New York Times* [Late New York Edition] 8 N 6 '93

(Nov. 5) Jack Kevorkian, the so-called suicide doctor who has helped 19 severely ill people kill themselves in the Detroit area since 1990, was jailed today. The action was the culmination of Kevorkian's repeated challenges to authorities to take him into custody, which is his way to intensify a battle against a new Michigan law that makes assisting suicide a felony carrying a 4-year prison term. Kevorkian's lawyer said the 65-year-old retired pathologist would immediately begin carrying out his long-standing threat to starve himself to death rather than remain behind bars.

AIDS patients seek solace in suicide but many risk added pain in failure. Gina Kolata. *New York Times* [Late New York Edition] C1+ Je 14 '94

People with AIDS and their advocates say that almost everyone with the disease considers suicide, but the issue of assisted suicide is fraught with problems. The difficulties facing AIDS patients wishing to commit suicide are discussed.

Life is sacred. That's the easy part. Ronald Myles Dworkin. *The New York Times Magazine* 36+ My 16 '93

Americans could ease the terrible bitterness that exists over the issues of abortion and euthanasia by changing their collective view of these 2 great controversies. Both sides in these conflicts approach the issues from their own spiritual values. Few Americans reject the idea that life is sacred; instead, people disagree about how best to respect the inherent value of a human life. By acknowledging the nature of this disagreement, Americans with different spiritual values could accept freedom of choice without feeling morally compromised. This acceptance would stem from recognition that a government committed to personal integrity and freedom would be wrong to dictate how people should view the meaning of their own lives and deaths.

There's no simple suicide. Lisa Belkin. *The New York Times Magazine* 48–55+ N 14 '93

The Rev. Ralph Mero is the founder of Compassion in Dying, an organization that helps terminally ill patients end their lives. The organization—which has been called both heroic and heretical—instructs, rather than assists, people in taking their own lives. It is made up of nurses, doctors, social workers, and members of the clergy who will offer advice on lethal drug doses, counsel family members, convince wary doctors, and literally hold a person's hand at death. The group will not provide or administer the drugs, however. The suicide of Louise J., who Mero instructed, is discussed.

Rationing life. David J. Rothman. *The New York Review of Books* 39:32–7 Mr 5 '92

Several books on medical ethics have recently been published. These include analyses of the rationing of health care and personal accounts of a willingness to accept limits on how much should be done to prolong life. The writer reviews Who Lives? Who Dies? Ethical Criteria in Patient Selection, by John F. Kilner; Strong Medicine: The Ethical Rationing of Health Care, by Paul T. Menzel; What Kind of Life: The Limits of Medical Progress and Setting Limits: Medical Goals in an Aging Society, both by Daniel Callahan; Just Doctoring: Medical Ethics in the Liberal State, by Troyen A. Brennan; Patrimony: A True Story, by Philip Roth; Someday, by Andrew H. Malcolm; and Final Exit: The Practicalities of Self-Deliverance and Assisted Suicide for the Dying, by Derek Humphry.

The real Jack Kevorkian. Mark Hosenball. *Newsweek* 122:28–9 D 6 '93

Jack Kevorkian's advocacy of physician-assisted suicide is part of a broad campaign to change the American way of death. An early supporter of execution by lethal injection, Kevorkian has proposed that condemned convicts be allowed to volunteer for "painless" medical experiments that would begin while they were alive but eventually prove fatal. In an article in an obscure German journal, he appeared to suggest that experiments could be conducted on fetuses, infants, children under a certain agreed-upon age, and "all brain-dead, comatose, mentally incompetent, or otherwise completely uncommunicative individuals." Ethics professor Robert Levine of Yale Medical School asserts that such experiments would probably not yield significant information. The writer discusses Kevorkian's career as a pathologist, his views on the Nazi Holocaust, and his responses to his critics.

William Styron. *People Weekly* 34:86–7 D 31 '90–Ja 7 '91

Part of a special issue on the prominent people and events of 1990. Renowned novelist William Styron recounted his bout with clinical depression in Darkness Visible. The book, which became a best seller, described Styron's journey to the brink of suicide, and it gave hope to the many sufferers of clinical depression.

Love unto death. Karen S. Schneider. *People Weekly* 37:56–60+ Ja 20 '92

ABC will soon air the TV movie Last Wish, which is based on a book by NBC correspondent Betty Rollin. In the book, Rollin describes how she helped her mother, Ida, commit suicide in 1983. Rollin's mother had been suffering from ovarian cancer, and doctors said that she was too weak to endure the needed chemotherapy treatments. Ida asked her daughter for help in ending her life, and Rollin, who had earlier suffered from breast cancer, obtained pills that her mother took to commit suicide. Rollin, who handles assignments for NBC's Nightly News and Today programs, is the author of the introduction to Derek Humphry's best selling suicide manual, Final Exit.

The last battle. David Ellis. *People Weekly* 41:67–8 My 30 '94

Disabled Vietnam veteran Lewis Puller Jr., author of the Pulitzer Prize-winning autobiography Fortunate Son, committed suicide on May 11 in his Alexandria, Va., home. Puller lost parts of both legs after stepping on a mine during his service in Vietnam in 1968. His book chronicles his recovery from his injuries and from ensuing bouts of alcoholism and depression. In recent months, however, Puller fell back into the cycle of pain and addiction that he described in Fortunate Son. His death is another addition to the number of suicides by Vietnam veterans, which many veterans' groups believe is alarmingly high.

A good death? Jacob Sullum. *Reason* 23:8 My '91

The right to live entails the right to die. Laws are limited and should not inquire into the reasons and the methods employed by people who choose suicide. The decision to commit or aid a suicide should remain with the individual. The moral debate over euthanasia should be thrashed out by doctors, philosophers, and religious leaders, not by legislators. Three cases involving terminally ill patients whose suicides were assisted by doctors are discussed.

Death by prescription. Thomas Stephen Szasz. *Reason* 24:46–7 Ap '93

There is something fundamentally wrong with the notion that every person has "a right to die" and, by extension, with everything based on that notion. Human views of suicide encompass incompatible beliefs: The decision to end one's life is an integral part of the fundamental right to control one's fate, yet the decision also is symptomatic of mental disease whose presence justifies coercive psychiatric intervention. Instead of acknowledging the conflict between these beliefs, we have expanded the repertoire of medical procedures to encompass the acts of doctors who "assist" patients who want to kill themselves. Suicide prevention has been relegated to psychiatric treatments, while the facilitation of suicide is viewed as the province of medicine. Viewing suicide as a moral choice, and the physician's participation in it as meddling, is professional heresy.

The disease is adolescence. Douglas Foster. *Rolling Stone* 55–7+ D 9 '93

Adolescence has become a high-risk activity, with the number of preventable deaths among teenagers rising at an alarming rate. According to the experiences of Barbara Staggers, a physician at the Teen Clinic at Children's Hospital in Oakland, California, who conducts clinics at area high schools, a festering generational grievance cuts across differences of income, ethnic background, and particular trauma and places teens at risk for murder, alcohol and drug abuse, suicide, and car crashes. Three-quarters of the deaths of people from ages 10 to 24 occur from such preventable causes, although HIV infection is spreading among the young as well. The risk of being shot to death has doubled in the last decade for people aged 15 to 19. Staggers believes that the most effective treatment for the ills that threaten teens today is one-on-one contact with a caring adult. Staggers's work is described.

Medicide: new humanism or old euthanasia? *Society* 29:4–38 Jl/Ag '92

A cover story examines medicide and terminally ill patients' right to die. Articles discuss the moral implications of suicide and doctor assisted death, Jack Kevorkian's suicide machine and his views on planned death, Kevorkian's justification for assisted suicide, the professional responsibilities of doctors involved with terminally ill patients who want to die, the legal implications of euthanasia, and the costs and benefits of assisted suicide.

The paradoxes of rational death. Robert Laurence Barry. *Society* 29:25–8 Jl/Ag '92

Part of a cover story on medicide. Jack Kevorkian's defense of the rationality and moral goodness of assisted suicide is unethical and potentially dangerous. Suicide violates the sanctity of human life, and though Kevorkian might argue that it can end the intolerable suffering of some terminal patients, such suffering is not morally proportionate to the evil of deliberate killing. Moreover, most analysts believe that suicide is not a rational choice, as Kevorkian insists, but one usually made in response to feelings of guilt, rejection, depression, isolation, failure, and self hatred. The liberal suicide policies that Kevorkian endorses would allow doctors to manipulate the vulnerable or unwanted into self assassination and would undermine the values of the medical profession and the trust between doctor and patient. The best answer to suffering is not suicide but charity, care, and understanding. Historical perspectives on suicide are discussed.

Masks of autonomy. John J. Conley. *Society* 29:11–15 Jl/Ag '92

Part of a cover story on medicide. Jack Kevorkian insists that the key value in his defense of active euthanasia is personal autonomy, but his views reveal instead the growing disvalue placed upon the terminally ill in American society. Kevorkian's enthusiastic support for the assisted suicide of terminal patients disregards familial, religious, ethical, and legal concerns surrounding the practice and focuses almost exclusively on the benefits to be gained from organ donations and experimental opportunities provided by those who choose to die. The cavalier acceptance of medicide by Kevorkian and other supporters· of the practice reflects a society in which the sick are unsupportable burdens; the desire for death among terminally ill patients is a result of this exclusion. The hospice movement, which offers an alternative environment of support to the terminally ill, is discussed.

Dignity, choice, and care. William Maxwell McCord. *Society* 29:20–4 Jl/Ag '92

Part of a cover story on medicide. Planned or assisted suicide can provide a dignified affirmation of liberty in the face of brutal circumstances. Patients who choose to assert control over their final suffering or death infuse an often formless reality with uniquely human meaning and compassion. Planned suicide can be a justified response to the intolerable burden that life represents for some terminally ill patients, but safeguards against interference by doctors and the state must be established to prevent abuses of assisted suicide. Public policy should prevent state authority from blocking an individual's right to die because this power would lead to state decisions on who is fit to live. Moreover, physicians, though necessary in an advisory capacity, should not be involved directly in ending life. The suicide traditions of several cultures are described, and the Ramsey Colloquium's Always to Care, Never to Kill: A Declaration on Euthanasia is discussed.

"I wanted to die": teens & suicide. Elizabeth Karlsberg. *'Teen* 37:56+ Ag '93

Each year, more than 100,000 people between the ages of 10 and 24 attempt suicide, and more than 6,000 of these young people are successful in their attempts. According to Charlotte Ross, founding director of the Suicide Prevention and Crisis Center of San Mateo County, California, suicide is the second leading cause of death for people in this age group. Two teenagers who survived suicide attempts share their stories.

Teen suicide: real life stories. Elizabeth Karlsberg. *'Teen* 35:24+ Ap '91

Teen suicide is a widespread problem. The statistics are sobering: suicide among young people has tripled since 1950, more than 100,000 people between the ages of 10 and 24 attempt suicide every year, and about 6,000 die as a result. If unreported cases were included in the statistics, suicide would rank as the primary cause of death for this age group. Depression usually precedes thoughts of suicide, with people who are depressed eventually coming to see suicide as their only option. Many adolescents, however, lose sight of the fact that sadness and pain won't last forever.

Generally, depression comes from a sense of loss. Talking things out can sometimes help teens avoid considering suicide. Stories from teens who have overcome thoughts of suicide are provided, myths and facts about suicide are discussed, suicide warning signs are described, and sources of help for teens experiencing suicidal thoughts are listed.

A swift route to suicide. *Time* 142:89 N 15 '93

A study by New York City's Cornell Medical Center raises the possibility that former Hemlock Society president Derek Humphry's controversial book Final Exit may increase the number of successful suicides among physically healthy people. The paper notes that in the year following the publication of the book, which suggests ways in which terminally ill patients can kill themselves quickly and easily, the number of suicides using one of the book's proposed methods increased 30 percent. The results of the study will be published in the New England Journal of Medicine.

Choosing death. *Time* 141:21 F 22 '93

The parliament of the Netherlands has approved the world's most liberal rules on euthanasia and doctor-assisted suicide. Both practices will remain technically illegal, but doctors will not be prosecuted if they notify coroners of their actions and follow established rules. Among other requirements, the patient must be mentally competent, must be suffering unbearable pain, and must request euthanasia repeatedly. The doctor must consult a second physician before complying with such a request.

Assigning the blame for a young man's suicide. Bonnie Angelo. *Time* 138:12+ N 18 '91

Ethel and Alan Adelman, the mother and brother of Adrian Adelman, claim that Adrian was depressed and killed himself by following instructions in the best selling suicide manual Final Exit, and they blame the book's author, Derek Humphry, for their tragedy. In an interview, they comment on their belief that Adrian would still be alive if he had not read Final Exit, their anger at Humphry, Adrian's depression and thoughts of suicide, directions in the book that Adrian followed, the toxicologist's report, their thoughts on assisted suicide and euthanasia, and the popularity of Final Exit.

Do-it-yourself death lessons. William A. Henry. *Time* 138:55 Ag 19 '91

Author Derek Humphry has written Final Exit, a manual for committing suicide. The book includes such information as charts on lethal dosages of prescription drugs, advice on how to asphyxiate oneself, and the pros and cons of cyanide, and it exhorts doctors and nurses to actively aid terminally ill patients in taking their own lives. Humphry says that people want to control their dying and that his book is a comfort to those who want to escape from the world if they are suffering unbearably. Some critics contend that his book may encourage suicide among unstable people, but Humphry distinguishes between "rational" suicide, undertaken by those who are irreversibly handicapped or terminally ill, and "emotional" suicide by those who are depressed, of which he disapproves. Humphry, the executive director of the Hemlock Society, a group whose motto is "Death with Dignity," has written three previous books on the subject and has assisted three family members in ending their lives.

Sisters of mercy. David Van Biema. *Time* 141:42–4 My 31 '93

Part of a cover story on the work of Jack Kevorkian. On May 15, 1992, Sue Weaver of Michigan committed suicide with the assistance of physician Jack Kevorkian. The article chronicles Weaver's battles with multiple sclerosis, her decision to ask for Kevorkian's help, Kevorkian's interviews with Weaver and her family, the day and circumstances of the suicide, and the thoughts of Weaver's family after her death.

Embracing the night. Miriam Horn. *U.S. News & World Report* 116:40–1 Ap 25 '94

The article recounts a dying woman's decision to enlist the help of Compassion in Dying, an organization that supported and advised her in her decision to commit suicide.

Getting help for depressed teenagers. *USA Today* [Periodical] 122:2 D '93

Roland Ciaranello of Stanford University Medical Center recommends that teenage depression be treated with drug and/or counseling therapy. Such treatment can often be crucial to success in school, a productive life, and even the prevention of suicide. While the cause of teenage depression is not clear, it is thought to be similar to adult depression, which most current theories ascribe to biochemical factors. In the case of adolescent depression, however, symptoms appear earlier in life because of a more acute internal chemical imbalance.

Angel of death: the trial of the suicide doctor. Ron Rosenbaum. *Vanity Fair* 54:146–51+ My '91

Dr. Jack Kevorkian, who helped Alzheimer's patient Janet Adkins commit suicide in 1990, has long questioned the way doctors deal with the agony of the dying. A pathologist and author of many books, Kevorkian created a device in 1989 that offers patients a swift and painless way to kill themselves. The patient touches a button that releases sodium pentothal into a vein, rendering him unconscious, whereupon a solution of potassium chloride stops his heart. The machine blurs the line between passive euthanasia, a medically sanctioned activity in which doctors withdraw life saving technology, and active euthanasia, a forbidden activity in which doctors induce death. Adkins was the only person to use the device. First-degree murder charges against Kevorkian were dismissed in 1990, but a Michigan judge has permanently barred him from using any device to assist a person in committing suicide. Kevorkian's attorney is appealing the ruling.

Suicide and attempted suicide. A.J.F.M. Kerkhof, *World Health* 18–20 Mr/Ap '94

Part of an issue on stress. Individual character traits and social influences contribute to suicide and attempted suicide. Most people who commit suicide have histories of emotional problems such as depression, anxiety, unhappy relationships, drug or alcohol abuse, problems with relatives, or feelings of loneliness or guilt. In many cases, their childhoods are marred by divorce, loss of a parent, sexual abuse, domestic violence, or parental alcohol abuse. Suicide rates also vary between different countries and population groups, suggesting the influence of social and cultural factors. It is especially prevalent among powerless groups such as young women, the uneducated, the unemployed, the disabled, and the divorced and separated. Suicide prevention programs must encourage enlightened attitudes toward mental illness so that those at risk of suicide will seek help.